T0381450

.

The Gospel According to

Esther

A Daily Devotional

DENISE A. ISAACS

WESTBOW
P R E S S®
A DIVISION OF THOMAS NELSON
& ZONDERVAN

Scripture taken from the King James Version of the Bible.

THE HOLY BIBLE, NEW INTERNATIONAL VERSION®,
NIV® Copyright © 1973, 1978, 1984, 2011 by Biblica, Inc.®
Used by permission. All rights reserved worldwide.

WestBow Press books may be ordered through booksellers or by contacting:

WestBow Press
A Division of Thomas Nelson & Zondervan
1663 Liberty Drive
Bloomington, IN 47403
www.westbowpress.com
1 (866) 928-1240

ISBN: 978-1-9736-5172-7 (sc)
ISBN: 978-1-9736-5173-4 (e)

Library of Congress Control Number: 2019900720

Print information available on the last page.

WestBow Press rev. date: 05/15/2019

Dedication

To my Lord and Savior Jesus Christ
and to his bride, the church.

Introduction

"Truly you are a God who has been hiding himself, the God and Savior of Israel" (Isaiah 45:15 NIV).

In the Book of Esther, there is no mention of God, the Holy Spirit or prayer. On the surface, there is nothing spiritual about the book. It seems to be a short historical account of the persecution of the Jews and their subsequent victory over their enemies.

In *The Gospel According to Esther* we will see the *hidden* story: the history of the human race as it is portrayed in the Bible. Scriptures from Genesis to Revelation tell this exciting story of a magnificent and loving God wanting to have a relationship with the people he created. The creation, the fall of humanity, the death and resurrection of Christ are just a few of the events covered. The overall theme of the book: God is preparing a bride for his Son.

The biblical events and stories are not necessarily in chronological order and are presented briefly; you may want to do a more in-depth study on your own. Also, if you are not familiar with the story of Esther; it will help you to read the Book of Esther (from your Bible) first. *The Gospel According to Esther* may be read as a "book" or as a daily devotional.

The main people in the Esther story are listed below, together with the person(s) they represent in the hidden story. Each verse or phrase of Esther is written out individually with its corresponding verse(s) that tell the other story. The phrase or verse in Esther being expounded upon is in italics.

THE MAIN CHARACTERS

King Xerxes—God

Queen Vashti—Eve, the human race

Mordecai—Jesus Christ, Son of God

Haman—Satan

Hegai, eunuchs—Holy Spirit

Esther—bride of Christ

Day 1

"This is what happened during the time of Xerxes" (Esther 1:1 NIV).

"One day is with the Lord as a thousand years, and a thousand years as one day" (2 Peter 3:8 KJV).

Time is an earth concept; God is timeless and eternal. We are limited by time, but God is not. We see things as they develop—minute by minute, hour by hour, day by day, year by year. But God sees the big picture. When God created the earth, the sun, the moon and the stars, he set into motion a sequence of time. The earth rotates once around its axis, and we have a day. The earth makes one revolution around the sun, and we have a year. People in ancient times used to think that the earth was the center of the universe; we still have a problem with that. We—as people—think we are the center of the universe, and everything revolves around us. But the truth is, the Son of God is the center of the universe, and everything revolves around him.

Prayer: Lord, be the center of my universe, and let my life revolve around you. Amen

Day 2

"The Xerxes who ruled over 127 provinces" (Esther 1:1 NIV).

"For God is the King of all the earth" (Psalm 47:7 KJV).

King Xerxes represents God. The 127 provinces represent Genesis 1:27 (KJV): "God created man in his own image … male and female." Esther 1:1 interpreted: This is what happened during the time that God ruled over the people he created. (See the Introduction.)

We are created in his image—an expression of himself but in bodily form. Each of us is made with a body, a soul, and a spirit. We, like God, have feelings, thoughts, and reasoning. But we are separate identities. We are not God, but beings created by him. We are above the animal and plant life. On earth we are at the top of the food chain, so to speak. We are God's crown jewels—priceless in his eyes.

But we have our limits; God made us that way. He also gave us free will; we have the ability to choose. This is the weak link in the chain, but more on that later. Since we were made with a limited capacity of body and mind, we need a higher being who provides guidance and wisdom as well as the very life force that keeps us breathing and functioning. (See Acts 17:28.) And that higher being is God—Father, Son, and Holy Spirit.

Prayer: God, you made us in your image, may we reflect you. Amen

Day 3

"Stretching from India to Cush" (Esther 1:1 NIV).
"His kingdom rules over all" (Psalm 103:19 NIV).

God's rule and authority encompasses all that exists. His kingdom rules over everything on earth, in the universe and in heaven. Lesser kingdoms of this world come and go. Kings and leaders, no matter how great they are, rule only for a time, and then they are gone. God and his kingdom last forever.

Not only does he rule over everything but he is also everywhere. If we ascend to heaven or descend to hell, he is there. If we climb the highest mountain or go into the depths of the sea, he is there. If we travel to the farthest corner of the earth, he is there. If we go to the outermost star in the cosmos, he is there. (See Psalms 10:16, 139:7-10.)

God rules over all, but he is not a tyrant or a bully. He rules in love because he is love. (See 1 John 4:16.) He is just, holy, right and true. His kingdom stands strong and unshakable—never to be overthrown by any other power or authority.

Prayer: "For thine is the kingdom, and the power, and the glory, for ever. Amen" (Matthew 6:13 KJV).

Day 4

"For in him we live, and move, and have our being" (Acts 17:28 KJV).

God, who made everything in the world, is ruler over all, and doesn't live in manmade buildings—as if we could contain him there. He doesn't need our help—as if he lacked anything of substance. Instead, he gives us life and everything. He populated the whole earth, starting with one person. He made nations and decided where they would be and when they would exist.

God engineered all this so we would look for him and possibly find him, for he is not far away. God understood our fixation on idols in the past. But now he requires all people to repent of their foolishness and turn to him, for he is the true God. One day all will be judged by him—the one who was raised from the dead—even Jesus Christ, the Son of God. (See Acts 17:24-31.)

God has given us as humans the capacity for acquiring knowledge and gaining wisdom, because he is the source of all wisdom and knowledge. But if people try to use the information and the knowledge of the world without going to the source, God, the outcome is faulty and unreliable. Sometimes the means we use to fix a problem only create more problems. The answers to the problems in this world can only be found in him and his wisdom.

Prayer: God, you are everything we need; may you be all that we desire. Amen

Day 5

"At that time King Xerxes reigned from his royal throne in the citadel of Susa" (Esther 1:2 NIV).

"The LORD'S throne is in heaven" (Psalm 11:4 KJV).

Susa represents heaven.

God reigns from his royal throne in heaven. God created the heavens. "The heavens, are the LORD"S: but the earth [has] he given to the children of men" (Psalm 115:16 KJV). It seems there are three heavens. The first heaven is the sky above us—the earth's atmosphere, where the birds and the planes fly. The second heaven is where the sun, the moon, the stars are. And the third heaven is where God and his angels and the heavenly beings live.

Paul the apostle said he was "caught up to the third heaven"—either in his body or in his spirit—where he received "visions and revelations of the Lord" (2 Corinthians 12:1-2 KJV).

The Lord says heaven is his throne, and the earth is his footstool. Because he sits high above the earth, we look like grasshoppers to him. (See Isaiah 66:1, 40:22.)

Heaven is a place we can look forward to going to after we die if we have put our faith in God's Son, Jesus. This hope helps us in our daily lives; it gives us a purpose.

Prayer: Lord, thank you that someday we will join you in heaven because of Jesus. Amen

Day 6

"And in the third year of his reign" (Esther 1:3 NIV).

"For there are three that bear record in heaven, the Father, the Word [Son], and the Holy [Spirit]: and these three are one" (1 John 5:7 KJV).

The third, or the number three, represents the Trinity: Father, Son, and Holy Spirit.

In Genesis 1:1-2 (KJV) we read: "In the beginning God created the heaven and the earth. And the earth was without form, and void; and darkness was upon the face of the deep. And the Spirit of God moved upon the face of the waters." Jesus, the Word, was there also with God, the Father, and the Holy Spirit. "In the beginning was the Word, and the Word was with God, and the Word was God. The same was in the beginning with God. All things were made by him; and without him was not anything made that was made" (John 1:1-3 KJV). From these verses, we see the Trinity—Father, Son, and Holy Spirit—all involved in the creation of the earth.

Just as the earth was dark and without life, we are in darkness and without life because of sin, until the Spirit of God comes to us. Jesus created all things—he brought life to the planet. And because he was sacrificed (killed) and shed his blood on the cross for our sins, he brings life to those who believe in him.

Prayer: Thank you—Father, Son, and Holy Spirit—that you work together in harmony to accomplish your plans and purposes. Amen

Day 7

"He gave a banquet for all his nobles and officials. The military leaders of Persia and Media, the princes, and the nobles of the provinces were present" (Esther 1:3 NIV).

"The morning stars sang together and all the angels shouted for joy" (Job 38:7 NIV).

The nobles and officials at the banquet represent the heavenly beings celebrating all the things the Lord has created.

In Job 38-41, the Lord talks about his creation to Job. He tells Job that he sets the boundaries for the sea so that its waves can only go so far. He puts the stars in their places. He sends the lightning and the rain and has authority over the snow and the hail. The Lord instructs Job about the lion and the goat, the ostrich and the hawk, the horse and the ox, and many other things. God says he is the one who gives wisdom and understanding to human hearts and minds. Job is humbled after hearing of God's mighty power and intimate knowledge of his creation.

You may want to read Genesis 1 and Job 38-41 so you can get a fresh glimpse of the Creator, God. Take a few minutes to think about his greatness. When you do this, it helps put your concerns in perspective. A God this big and powerful can certainly take care of your needs.

Prayer: Lord, your wisdom and knowledge are beyond anything we as humans can comprehend. We are awed by your greatness. Amen

"For a full 180 days" (Esther 1:4 NIV).

"For by him were all things created, that are in heaven, and that are in earth, visible and invisible" (Colossians 1:16 KJV).

"For a full 180 days." (180 = half, 360 = whole, as in a circle.)

Full means both halves—the spiritual realm and the natural, physical realm. The visible is the physical realm we see and the invisible is the spiritual realm, unseen by natural eyes. Just because God and the spiritual realm cannot be seen doesn't mean they aren't real. The wind is invisible but no one doubts that it exists. John compares the Holy Spirit to the wind; you can hear the sound of it but can't tell where it's going or what it's going to do. (See John 3:8.)

We can't see the angels of God, usually, but God does sometimes allow us to see them. We can't see the fallen angels—demons—but they are real also. The forces of evil (the devil and his demons), are in conflict with the spiritual forces of good (God and his holy angels). They are in a battle for the souls of people; this battle began with Adam and Eve in the Garden.

God is greater than the evil in the world. Those who choose to be on his side are on the winning side!

Prayer: Thank you, Lord, that we believe you are real even though we can't see you. Please open the eyes and hearts of others so that they may believe. Amen

Day 9

"He displayed the vast wealth of his kingdom" (Esther 1:4 NIV).

"The silver is mine, and the gold is mine," says the Lord. (Haggai 2:8 KJV).

As early as the second chapter of the Bible we hear about gold—and it was good gold. (See Genesis 2:11-12.) Generations later, "Abram [Abraham] was very rich in cattle, in silver, and in gold" (Genesis 13:2 KJV). The Lord told Moses to take an offering from the people for the building of the tabernacle and its furnishings. The first two items that the Lord asked for were gold and silver. (See Exodus 25:1-3.)

God declares that all the animals in the forest are his and the cattle on a thousand hills belong to him. The whole world belongs to him—everything in it. (See Psalm 50:10; 24:1.)

In Leviticus 25:23, the Lord says he owns the land and that the people who live there are foreigners and strangers.

Jesus told two parables about a man who owned a vineyard and in each it is assumed that the landowner is God. (See Matthew 20:1-16, 21:33-41)

The world and everything in it is the Lord's; he made it. That pretty much covers the riches of his kingdom on this earth. Today, wealth is still defined by silver, gold, cattle and land. God put these things here for us, but they really belong to him. He gave us all these things to use and enjoy.

Prayer: Lord, you own the earth; help us as tenants to take good care of it. Amen

Day 10

"And the splendor and glory of his majesty" (Esther 1:4 NIV).

"Yours, LORD, is the greatness and the power and the glory and the majesty and the splendor, for everything in heaven and earth is yours. Yours, LORD, is the kingdom; you are exalted as head over all" (1 Chronicles 29:11 NIV).

If you go outside at night away from the city lights and look up into the sky you can see that "the heavens declare the glory of God" (Psalm 19:1 KJV). The stars are shining with his glory.

The mountains, too, are awesome in their splendor. And the ocean is vast and majestic. These are God's glorious creations and they are only a small reflection of him. The whole of God's glory and splendor are beyond our understanding.

When Jesus was on the earth, he gave three of his disciples a glimpse of his glorious state when they were up on a mountain. For a short time, he was transformed before their eyes; his face was bright like the sun and his clothing was white as snow. (See Matthew 17:2.)

In the future age, we won't need the sun and the stars to give us light because the glory of the Lord will be the light and there won't be any night.

Prayer: "To the only wise God our [Savior], be glory and majesty, dominion and power, both now and ever. Amen" (Jude v. 25 KJV).

Day 11

"When these days were over" (Esther 1:5 NIV).

"The heavens and the earth were finished" (Genesis 2:1 KJV).

There was now light and dark called day and night. The water was gathered together to make seas. In the seas, there were fish and whales and other aquatic life. The ground grew grass and plants and trees (with fruit). There were animals big and small. In the sky, was the sun, the moon and the stars.

And there was a man, Adam. He was given the job of taking care of the garden. He also named the animals. But there wasn't anyone he could relate to as a person; so the Lord made Eve as a helper and companion for him.

God looked over all that he had created: the stars in the sky, the plant and animal life and the people he had made in his image and he was pleased; it was good, very good. (See Genesis 1-2.)

Prayer: Lord, when we look at the beautiful creation you have made, indeed it is very good. Amen

Day 12

"The king gave a banquet" (Esther 1:5 NIV).

"The LORD God made all kinds of trees grow out of the ground—trees that were pleasing to the eye and good for food" (Genesis 2:9 NIV).

The Lord provided a banquet for Adam and Eve and their future offspring to feast on. The people he made had all that they needed to live a good life in the Garden of Eden. God had fellowship with them and things were going along smoothly. God had the perfect means to show off his glory, power and goodness; through these humans he had created. This was Plan A, but as we will soon see a Plan B will be needed.

Jesus told his followers this story or parable: "The kingdom of heaven is like a king who prepared a wedding banquet for his son" (Matthew 22:2 NIV). In this parable, the king represents God, and his son, the Son of God, Jesus. This parable depicts the history of the human race and is the parallel story for this devotional. (There's a summary of this parable on Day 13.)

Prayer: Lord, you want to have fellowship with the people you created. Thank you for making this possible through your Son. Amen

Day 13

"The king gave a banquet" (Esther 1:5 NIV).

Here's a summary of the parable of the wedding banquet in Matthew 22:1-14:

A king prepared a wedding dinner for his son. He sent out servants to remind the invited guests to come to the dinner. They declined to come. Later he sent more servants out to tell the guests the dinner was ready. But they were too busy to come—one was needed on the farm; another had to tend the store. The others treated his servants shamefully, even killed them. The king was furious. He commanded his army to destroy those wicked people and burn down their city. Those he originally invited didn't deserve his dinner.

He sent the servants out again and told them to gather up anybody they saw—good or bad. The servants did this and he had a full house. The king noticed a guest there who was not dressed in wedding clothes—he was thrown out in the dark. "For many are called, but few are chosen" (Matthew 22:14 KJV).

The Lord wants us at his banquet. But we must make time for him now. We need to set God as our top priority. Our present quality of life and certainly our future in eternity is at stake. Let's take the time.

Prayer: Thank you, God, for your love for us—you want us at your banquet. Help us to take the time to know you. Amen

"Lasting seven days" (Esther 1:5 NIV).

"And on the seventh day God ended his work" (Genesis 2:2 KJV).

The number seven is said to symbolize completion. God created the world and rested the seventh day; in seven days all was completed. In this devotional, the seven-day banquet represents the complete history of mankind on the earth: beginning with Adam and Eve in the Garden and continuing to the marriage supper of the Lamb and the Garden in the new earth. Stories from throughout the Bible will be woven into the story of Esther.

In your own life you can probably think of your own "seven days" of completion. It could be that you completed your schooling or you completed a big project at work. Perhaps you look at your seven days of completion as the time you finished raising your kids and now you are an empty nester. Or you may have changed jobs or careers, and now you are in a new seven-day cycle. Let's trust God and look to him to guide us during these times.

Prayer: God, you are sovereign; your plans will be carried out and come to completion. Amen

Day 15

"In the enclosed garden of the king's palace" (Esther 1:5 NIV).

"A garden inclosed is my sister, my spouse" and "I am come into my garden, my sister, my spouse" (Song of Solomon 4:12, 5:1 KJV).

As in the verses above, "sister" and "spouse" speak of a close relationship. (See Mark 3:35; Revelation 19:7.) The "enclosed garden" represents the church, the bride (spouse) of Christ. (The church: those who have a personal relationship with God through his Son, Jesus.)

"The king's palace" represents where God, the King, lives in heaven. The enclosed garden in heaven also represents where the church lives spiritually now: God "raised us up ... and made us sit together in heavenly places in Christ Jesus" (Ephesians 2:6 KJV). "Your life is hid with Christ in God" (Colossians 3:2 KJV). This is the spiritual realm; but at the same time, believers are living their lives in the natural, physical world.

Think of it this way, the enclosed garden is a place and a people; just like when Christians say they are going to church (a place), and they are the church (a people).

Enclose means to surround. Psalm 125:2 (NIV) says, "as the mountains surround Jerusalem, so the Lord surrounds his people both now and forevermore." God's people are surrounded by his love and care. "He that [lives] in the secret [enclosed] place of the most High shall abide under the shadow of the Almighty" (Psalm 91:1 KJV). We are safe in him.

Prayer: Thank you, Lord, that we are surrounded by your presence and kept in your care. Amen

Day 16

"In the enclosed garden of the king's palace" (Esther 1:5 NIV).

"Now the LORD God had planted a garden in the east, in Eden; and there he put the man he had formed" (Genesis 2:8 NIV).

The enclosed garden also represents the enclosed garden in Eden, a type of "heaven" on earth.

"And the LORD God formed man of the dust of the ground, and breathed into his nostrils the breath of life; and man became a living soul" (Genesis 2:7 KJV). God put the man, Adam in the garden in Eden to take care of it. The Lord provided many trees for food. Also, in the middle of the garden stood the tree of life and the tree of the knowledge of good and evil. God told Adam that he could eat from any tree in the garden except the tree of the knowledge of good and evil. If he ate from that tree he would die.

God saw that Adam was alone. So he put him to sleep, took one of his ribs and closed him up. From the rib he made a woman, Eve. Adam and Eve were as God made them, naked, but they were not embarrassed at this. (See Genesis 2.)

Prayer: Father, thank you for the Bible that tells us how things were in the beginning. Amen

Day 17

"For all the people from the least to the greatest who were in the citadel of Susa" (Esther 1:5 NIV).

"And they shall come from the east, and from the west, and from the north, and from the south, and shall sit down in the kingdom of God" (Luke 13:29 KJV).

This future feast with God is for those who have responded to the invitation. God gives the invitation to all to come to his banquet in the enclosed garden in heaven. Young or old, rich or poor, educated or uneducated; the least in the eyes of others or the most famous: all are equal in his sight and loved by him.

When Jesus was on the earth he associated with the less desirable people of his time and got criticized for it. He ate with tax collectors, who were despised by most people. He approached lepers, who were not allowed to make physical contact with anyone. His healing touch made them whole, so they could be restored to the community and be with their family and friends again. These outcasts were loved by him and were welcome to be part of his kingdom.

The people attending the Lord's banquet will come from different countries, different cultures and different backgrounds, but they will all have one thing in common: they followed God.

Prayer: Lord, "people from the least to the greatest" here on earth will be with you in heaven. You love all people. Help us to follow your example. Amen

Day 18

"The garden had hangings of white and blue linen, fastened with cords of white linen and purple material to silver rings on marble pillars" (Esther 1:6 NIV).

"And let them make me a sanctuary; that I may dwell among them" (Exodus 25:8 KJV).

There are some similarities in Esther 1:6 above, to the sanctuary or tabernacle in Exodus 26. The curtains of the tabernacle were to be made of linen, with the color scheme of blue, purple and red; other articles were made out of silver and gold. God told Moses to have the people make him a tabernacle so that he could be with them. This is the place where God would meet with his people.

The tabernacle on earth was a copy of the heavenly tabernacle. (See Hebrews 8:5.)

Believers in Christ are God's tabernacle or temple where his Spirit dwells, it is a sacred place. We need to protect it. (See 1 Corinthians 3:16-17.) As much as possible we need to guard our temple from evil influences that come from what we see and hear. For example, we should be selective in choosing what we view, read, listen to and where we go. We can pray and ask God to give us wisdom and discernment in this, so we can keep our temple holy.

Prayer: Father, come and dwell with us in the tabernacle of our hearts and keep us pure so that someday we may join you in your tabernacle in heaven. Amen

Day 19

"There were couches of gold and silver on a mosaic pavement of porphyry, marble, mother-of-pearl and other costly stones" (Esther 1:6 NIV).

"The foundations of the wall of the city were garnished with ... precious stones" (Revelation 21:19 KJV).

The couches and pavement in Esther 1:6, resembles the New Jerusalem with its many jewels. "And the building ... was of jasper: and the city was pure gold. ... And the foundations ... were garnished with all manner of precious stones. ... And the twelve gates were twelve pearls ... and the street of the city was pure gold" (Revelation 21:18, 19, 21 KJV). "And I John saw the holy city, new Jerusalem, coming down from God out of heaven, prepared as a bride adorned for her husband" (Revelation 21:2 KJV).

What God has for our future is way beyond our human understanding. Babies in the womb may think that what they experience in those few months is what life is all about. Then they are born and wow—life is so different.

When we are born again spiritually, (see John 3) we have a new world opened up to us again. When we die or Jesus returns to take his people home, we will have a new experience again. God is so creative; perhaps this cycle of new continues on and on throughout eternity.

Prayer: God, you are so awesome. We await the discovery of what you have for us. Amen

"Wine was served" (Esther 1:7 NIV).

"The Lamb slain from the foundation of the world" (Revelation 13:8 KJV).

The wine being served represents the blood of Christ shed for us. (As in Holy Communion the wine represents Christ's blood.)

God ordained that blood be shed for the forgiveness of sins. (See Hebrews 9:22.) It is because of the sacrifice of Jesus on the cross that God pardons our sins. The death and resurrection of Christ is the whole of Christianity. (See 1 Corinthians 1:23, 2:2, 15:20.)

We can't make ourselves good enough to meet God's standard of holiness. Faith in Christ and his blood is the means by which we are reconciled to God.

Prayer: Thank you, Lord Jesus, for giving your blood so that we could be forgiven. Amen

Day 21

"In goblets of gold" (Esther 1:7 NIV).
"We have this treasure in jars of clay" (2 Corinthians 4:7 NIV).

Wine in goblets of gold represents Christ in us.

The Lord has made us—he is the potter and we are the clay. (See Isaiah 64:8.)

We are the clay cups that hold a treasure. The saints of God may look the same as others on the outside, but inside we have a treasure, Christ Jesus.

God sees us as valuable "goblets of gold" because of the sacrifice of his Son. Our trials and troubles in life are like a refining process to purify us, as gold is purified.

"When he [has] tried me, I shall come forth as gold" (Job 23:10 KJV).

"[May] the trial of your faith, being more precious than of gold ... though it be tried with fire" give praise and glory to Jesus at his appearing. (1 Peter 1:7 KJV)

This purifying is a lifetime process. It is to make us holy as he is holy. (See 1 Peter 1:16.) "For by one sacrifice [Jesus Christ] he has made perfect forever those who are being made holy" (Hebrews 10:14 NIV). We are transformed from clay cups to gold goblets!

Prayer: God, help us as we are being refined to put our trust in you. May we believe that you are working in us for our good and for your glory. Amen

"Each one different from the other" (Esther 1:7 NIV).

"We have different gifts, according to the grace given to each of us" (Romans 12:6 NIV).

People are different from each other in personality, looks, strengths and weaknesses; but that is how God made us. Some people are outgoing and talkative, others are quiet. Some work well in groups, others prefer to work alone. Some love to care for children and others would rather care for older folks.

And as our physical body has different parts that work together for the good of the whole body, the "body of Christ" the church, should work together for the good of the whole. All types of gifts are needed in the church because there is a need to reach out to all types of people in the church and in the world.

And just because some gifts are more visible than others, that doesn't make them more valuable to God. In our body we have a heart and lungs; those are not seen but they are very necessary. But what is most important is that we use our gifts and callings out of a heart of love for God and others.

Prayer: Lord, help us to love and serve you with the gifts you have given us. Amen

Day 23

"And the royal wine was abundant" (Esther 1:7 NIV).

"It was not with perishable things such as silver or gold that you were redeemed ... but with the precious blood of Christ" (1 Peter 1:18-19 NIV).

Christ's blood (the royal wine) is abundant, more than enough to cover our sins. "In whom we have redemption through his blood, the forgiveness of sins, according to the riches of his grace" (Ephesians 1:7 KJV).

Jesus said, "I am come that they might have life, and that they might have it more abundantly" (John 10:10 KJV). In Christ we have many spiritual blessings. We have forgiveness of our sins and the restoration of our relationship with the heavenly Father. The Holy Spirit works in us and gives us power not to sin. We can tell the Lord our troubles and receive his comfort. He helps us make decisions and gives us direction from the Bible, the Holy Spirit, godly people or other sources he may lead us to. He gives us peace when we walk according to his plans. We have his Spirit to nudge us when we go astray, and get us back on track. We are loved unconditionally. And we have family—our brothers and sisters in Christ.

We can have a spiritually abundant life now and for all eternity.

Prayer: Thank you, God, for the abundance of spiritual blessings we have in Christ. Amen

Day 24

"In keeping with the king's liberality" (Esther 1:7 NIV).

"But my God shall supply all your need according to his riches in glory by Christ Jesus" (Philippians 4:19 KJV).

God is a generous God and provides for his people. For forty years God provided food and water for the Israelites in the desert; and their clothes and shoes didn't even wear out. (See Exodus 15-16; Deuteronomy 29:5.) God had ravens take bread and meat to the prophet Elijah twice a day. (See 1 Kings17:6.) Jesus fed thousands of people with a few fish and loaves of bread. (See Matthew 14:21.)

Jesus said for us not to worry about things like food to eat and clothes to wear. God takes care of the birds by feeding them and we mean more to him than the birds do. God dresses the flowers beautifully; he can dress us.

So, don't worry; worrying doesn't help anyway. Unbelievers fret because they don't know the Father like we do. Our heavenly Father knows what we need. If we put him first in our lives, he will see that we have food and clothes. And don't worry about tomorrow—he's got that covered, too. (See Matthew 6:25-34.)

God promises to supply all our need, not all our greed.

Prayer: Father, "give us this day our daily bread" (Matthew 6:11 KJV). Amen

Day 25

"By the king's command each guest was allowed to drink with no restrictions" (Esther 1:8 NIV).

"Work out your own salvation with fear and trembling" (Philippians 2:12 KJV).

We are not to put restrictions on others and judge the way they live for God; God will take care of them. (See Romans 14.). Each Christian is called to obey the Lord and walk out his own life according to the way God leads him personally; but his lifestyle should not contradict the written word of God.

Jesus said we were not to critically judge others. He told a story about a person wanting to take a speck of dust out of his brother's eye when there was a board in his own. Jesus said the man needed to first take the board out of his own eye and then he would be able to see to take the speck of dust out of his brother's eye. (See Matthew 7:1-5.)

May we look to Jesus for the way he wants us to live our own lives and pray for our brothers and sisters in the Lord that they will do the same.

Prayer: Father, help us not to judge others. Amen

Day 26

"For the king instructed all the wine stewards to serve each man what he wished" (Esther 1:8 NIV).

"If you remain in me, [Jesus said] and my words remain in you, ask whatever you wish, and it will be done for you" (John 15:7 NIV).

The goodness and grace of God are there for the asking. We can have as much of this royal wine (spiritual life in Christ) as we wish. We can be as close to God as we wish to be. God is always wanting to be with us. He loves us and wants a daily personal relationship with us. He wants us to stick close to him with his Word in us guiding our footsteps.

When we seek the Lord and call out to him, he hears us. "Draw [near] to God, and he will draw [near] to you" (James 4:8 KJV). God will respond to any whole-hearted effort we make to know him. When we listen to his voice and obey his commands, he will work in our lives and circumstances and reward us accordingly.

What are we wishing for? An easy life?
What are we wishing for? Wealth, power, fame?
What are we wishing for? Holiness, Christ-likeness?

Prayer: Lord, may our wishes be holy wishes turned into holy prayers for your glory. Amen

Day 27

Next, we see Queen Vashti's rebellion and the consequences. Vashti symbolizes the rebellion of Eve and the human race against a holy, loving God.

"Queen Vashti also gave a banquet for the women in the royal palace of King Xerxes" (Esther 1:9 NIV).

Queen Vashti represents Eve and lost humanity. She has her own banquet separate from the king. "For what do righteousness and wickedness have in common? Or what fellowship can light have with darkness?" (2 Corinthians 6:14 NIV).

In Genesis 3, Eve is tempted by a snake—Satan in disguise—to eat from the tree of the knowledge of good and evil, the tree God told them they must not eat from or they would die. Eve ate of the forbidden fruit because she thought it looked good and the snake promised it would make her wise like God, knowing good and evil.

She gave some to Adam to eat and he did. Then they were ashamed that they were naked, so they found fig leaves and sewed them together to make clothing.

This is how sin entered the world: Adam and Eve chose to decide for themselves what was right and wrong instead of trusting God's wisdom and limits.

Prayer: Lord, "lead us not into temptation, but deliver us from evil" (Matthew 6:13 KJV). Amen

Day 28

"On the seventh day, when King Xerxes was in high spirits from wine" (Esther 1:10 NIV).

"It is finished" Jesus said on the cross. (John 19:30 KJV).

Again this "seventh" day means completion; and the wine represents the blood of Christ. Jesus had completed the work the Father had for him to do; he laid down his life—shed his blood—to pay for the sins of all people. It is finished. God has done everything for our salvation. We need to only believe it and live it.

"For he [has] made him to be sin for us, who knew no sin; that we might be made the righteousness of God in him" (2 Corinthians 5:21 KJV).

He took on our sin and we take on his righteousness; that is quite an exchange. He laid down his life for us. In thankfulness, we need to lay down our lives for him. Jesus submitted to the will of the Father and we need to submit to the will of the Father. Jesus completed the assignment God had for him; we need to complete the assignments God has given us.

Prayer: God, you have given us so much, help us not to take it for granted but to give our lives to you in return. Amen

Day 29

"He commanded the seven eunuchs who served him—Mehuman, Biztha, Harbona, Bigtha, Abagtha, Zethar and Karkas" (Esther 1:10 NIV).

"The seven Spirits which are before his throne" (Revelation 1:4 KJV).

The seven eunuchs represent the seven Spirits.

The seven Spirits are not named here. In the Book of Revelation, it says the Lamb has "seven horns and seven eyes, which are the seven Spirits of God sent forth into all the earth" (Revelation 5:6 KJV). Seven means complete; therefore, Jesus possessed all the fulness of the Spirit.

There is a prophecy about Jesus in Isaiah 11:2 that does mention seven spirits:

1. The spirit of the Lord (Luke 4:18)
2. The spirit of wisdom (Ephesians 1:17)
3. The spirit of understanding (Luke 24:45)
4. The spirit of counsel (Psalm 73:24)
5. The spirit of might (Judges 14:6)
6. The spirit of knowledge (1 Corinthians 12:8)
7. The spirit of the fear of the Lord (2 Chronicles 19:7)

Prayer: Lord, may your church walk in the fulness of the Spirit. Amen

"To bring before him Queen Vasti" (Esther 1:11 NIV).

"And they heard the voice of the LORD God walking in the garden in the cool of the day: and Adam and his wife hid themselves from the presence of the LORD God amongst the trees of the garden" (Genesis 3:8 KJV).

The Lord wanted to visit with Adam and Eve but they were hiding. Sin separates us from God. We hide and he comes looking for us because he loves us. We were lost in sin and God sent his Son down to walk in the garden of this world and find us.

Jesus told a parable of a man with two sons. The younger son wanted his inheritance right away, so his father gave it to him. The son left. After spending his inheritance money foolishly supporting his sinful lifestyle; he decided to go home.

Even before he reached home, his father saw him. The father felt such a love for his son that he ran to him and hugged him. The son confessed to his father that he had sinned against him and against God. He said he wasn't worthy to be called his son. The father forgave him and responded by throwing him a party. His lost son was now found. (See Luke 15:11-32.)

This is how God the Father feels about us when we come home to him.

Prayer: Father, thank you for forgiving us and welcoming us home. Amen

Day 31

"Wearing her royal crown" (Esther 1:11 NIV).

You have made them a little lower than the angels and crowned them with glory and honor" (Psalm 8:5 NIV).

A crown represents authority. God gave humans the highest position in the earth; they had authority over everything in it. They were to take care of the plants and animals and fill the world with people. (See Genesis 1:28.)

After their sin, not only were Adam and Eve affected spiritually (their relationship with God was broken) and physically (their bodies were going to die); there were other consequences. The snake was cursed by God and would crawl on the ground from then on. God told Eve she would have pain in bearing children and her husband would dominate her.

Because Adam also ate the fruit, the ground was cursed and it would produce thorns and thistles and he would have to work hard to get food to grow for them to eat. When he died, he would return to the ground from which he was made. (See Genesis 2:7, 3:14-19.)

All of the earth was affected by their sin. (See Romans 8:19-22.)

Prayer: Father, we are still living with the consequences of Adam and Eve's fateful choice. Thank you, God that you made a way for us, in Christ. Amen

Day 32

"In order to display her beauty to the people and nobles, for she was lovely to look at" (Esther 1:11 NIV).

"I know what a beautiful woman you are" (Genesis 12:11 NIV).

Abram's wife Sarai was a beautiful woman. Because of a famine, Abram and Sarai went to live in Egypt for a time. As they entered Egypt, Abram told Sarai to tell the Egyptians that she was his sister. (Actually, she was his half-sister. See Genesis 20:12.) Abram was afraid a man would kill him and take beautiful Sarai as his wife.

The man and woman and all of God's creation were more beautiful than we can imagine; all was very good until sin entered the picture. Think about how beautiful the world would be today without violence, greed, sickness, war, pain and death.

One day it will be different, but for now we live in a broken world and only God can fix it. And he will fix it, in his time. God will "create new heavens and a new earth: and the former shall not be remembered, nor come into mind" (Isaiah 65:17 KJV).

Prayer: Thank you, God, that one day everything will be new and beautiful. Amen

Day 33

"But when the attendants delivered the king's command, Queen Vashti refused to come" (Esther 1:12 NIV).

"The LORD God called to the man, 'Where are you?'" (Genesis 3:9 NIV).

Soon after Adam and Eve had sinned against God by eating the fruit from the forbidden tree; the Lord was walking in the garden and he called out to them and asked where they were. Adam and Eve did not come when the Lord called because they had sinned and were ashamed. After they confessed, God made clothes for them from animal skins.

God provided the first animal sacrifice for the forgiveness of sin; later he provided Christ who became the ultimate sacrifice for sin. (See Genesis 3:8-21; Hebrews 10:12.)

In the parable of the banquet, the king sent his servants out to ask those who were invited to come, but they wouldn't come. Later, he sent other servants out to give the message that the food was ready and it was time to come to the marriage. But the guests paid little attention to the servants. They were busy and had other things to do. (See Matthew 22:3-5.)

God continues to call lost people, but many, like Queen Vashti, refuse to come.

Prayer: God, may you continue to work in the hearts of the lost, giving each another opportunity to come to you. Amen

"Then the king became furious and burned with anger" (Esther 1:12 NIV).

"God is angry with the wicked every day" (Psalm 7:11 KJV).

In the banquet story the king (who represents God) was furious, his invited guests would not come to his great feast. They also had attacked and killed the king's servants. So the king had his army destroy those people and set their city on fire. (See Matthew 22:6-7.)

Throughout the history of the Israelites, God was angry at his sinful, stubborn people because they refused to obey him and they mistreated and killed the prophets he sent to them. There are many stories of God disciplining them and then showing them his mercy and forgiveness. Even though they continued to stray, the Lord never gave up on them. But he did have a new tactic in mind: he would send his Son.

God hates sin! And as followers of God we should hate sin, too. We should love the person but hate the sin in them (and in us). We have already talked about sin destroying our relationship with God but sin also destroys or damages relationships among people. Families, friends, communities and countries—no one is immune to this epidemic, this fatal disease—sin.

Prayer: Great Physician, only you have the cure for this disease called sin. Please come and heal us. Amen

Day 35

"Since it was customary for the king to consult experts in matters of law and justice, he spoke with the wise men who understood the times" (Esther 1:13 NIV).

The Lord spoke to the prophet Daniel about the end times. He said, "Many shall be purified, and made white, and tried; but the wicked shall do wickedly: and none of the wicked shall understand; but the wise shall understand" (Daniel 12:10 KJV).

In the last days, the church will be purified, to be prepared as the bride of Christ. 1 Peter 4:17-18 (KJV) says, "For the time is come that judgment must begin at the house of God: and if it first begin at us, what shall the end be of them that obey not the gospel of God? And if the righteous scarcely be saved, where shall the ungodly and the sinner appear?"

Jesus said that the trouble during this time will be like nothing that has ever happened or will ever exist again. Those difficult days of great tribulation will be shortened or else no one would survive. God will cut them short for the sake of his chosen ones.

The wicked won't understand what is happening; but God's true followers will understand that these difficult times must come, and they will persevere to the end. Then the Lord will return and gather his people to himself.

Prayer: Father, may our faith not fail in our time of testing but be purified and made strong. Amen

"And were closest to the king—Karshena, Shethar, Admatha, Tarshish, Meres, Marsena and Memukan, *the seven nobles of Persia and Media who had special access to the king and were highest in the kingdom"* (Esther 1:14 NIV).

"The angel said to him, 'I am Gabriel. I stand in the presence of God'" (Luke 1:19 NIV).

The nobles represent the archangels—the highest-ranking angels of God, who have special access to the King. King Xerxes had seven nobles. (Again, we have the number 7.) The Bible mentions at least two archangels, Gabriel and Michael; there may be more.

In Daniel 8-9, Gabriel interpreted the visions the Lord had given Daniel. In Luke 1: Gabriel was sent by God to speak to Zechariah to tell him he would have a son; even though he and his wife were very old and had always been childless. This son was John the Baptist, the forerunner of Christ. He also visited Mary to tell her she would have a son, Jesus.

The archangel Michael was called on to help another angel deliver a message to Daniel. (See Daniel 10:13.) He also contended with the devil over Moses' body. (See Jude v. 9.) In Revelation 12:7-9, it says there was a war taking place in heaven and it was Michael and his angels who fought against the devil and his angels; the devil and his angels were cast out of heaven.

Prayer: Thank you, God, that you have mighty angels at your command. Amen

Day 37

*"According to law, what must be done to Queen Vashti?'
he asked. 'She has not obeyed the command of King Xerxes that
the eunuchs have taken to her'"* (Esther 1:15 NIV).

"For the wages of sin is death" (Romans 6:23 KJV).

The law of God says death is the penalty for sin. Adam
and Eve disobeyed the command of God by eating of the
fruit of the tree of the knowledge of good and evil. The Lord
said that if they ate from it they would die.

God says he doesn't experience any pleasure when the
wicked die; he desires instead that they turn from their evil
ways and live. (See Ezekiel 33:11.) God wants all to turn
from their sin and ask his forgiveness so that they may live
to know his love and goodness as well as receive eternal life
with him.

Some may come to Christ at the end of their lives.
When Jesus was on the cross there were two thieves also
being crucified. One of them feared God and asked Jesus to
not forget him when he claimed his kingdom. Jesus assured
him that that very day he would join him in Paradise. (See
Luke 23:40-43.)

Prayer: Lord, help us never to give up on others. As long as
they are alive, they have a chance to ask you for forgiveness
and receive the gift of salvation. Amen

"Then Memukan replied in the presence of the king and the nobles, *'Queen Vashti has done wrong, not only against the king but also against all the nobles and the peoples of all the provinces of King Xerxes'"* (Esther 1:16 NIV).

"By one man [and woman] sin entered into the world, and death by sin; and so death passed upon all" (Romans 5:12 KJV).

Eve sinned, then Adam sinned, and consequently all people. Eve had done wrong, not just against God, but against all the people who were to come after. The downward spiral happened quickly. In the very next chapter, Genesis 4, we read about two murders; Adam and Eve's son Cain killed his brother Abel, and another person was murdered by a descendant of Cain.

"For as by one man's disobedience many were made sinners, so by the obedience of one shall many be made righteous" (Romans 5:19 KJV.) This verse starts with the bad news—we are all sinners because one person messed up—but then it goes right into the good news—by the obedience of one person (Jesus Christ) we can be made righteous. This story has a rough beginning but a happy ending because God chose to rewrite it by inserting his Son into the plot. That changed everything. Now we can have a "happily ever after" kind of story.

Prayer: Thank you, God, for rewriting history. Your great love is amazing! Amen

Day 39

"For the queen's conduct will become known to all the women" (Esther 1:17 NIV).

The queen's conduct has been known (experienced) by all: "For all have sinned, and come short of the glory of God" (Romans 3:23 KJV).

The Pharisees and the teachers of the law—the religious leaders—brought a woman caught in adultery to Jesus; they wanted to see what he would do about it. They wanted to get him in trouble and discredit him in front of the crowd. In the law Moses gave them from God, it said she should be stoned. They continued to pester Jesus for an answer. Jesus told them that whoever had never sinned could be the first to throw a stone at her. Her accusers slipped away one by one. Jesus didn't condemn her but told her go and not sin anymore. (See John 8:2-11.)

The men who brought the woman to Jesus realized that they were sinners, too.

No matter how long we live as followers of Christ we will still need his grace and forgiveness.

Prayer: Father, we have sinned. We believe that Jesus paid the price for our sins on the cross. Please forgive us and make us clean. Amen

Day 40

"And so they will despise their husbands and say" (Esther 1:17 NIV).

"And as the ark of the LORD came into the city of David, Michal Saul's daughter looked through a window, and saw king David leaping and dancing before the LORD; and she despised him in her heart" (2 Samuel 6:16 KJV).

David's wife, Michal, was embarrassed to have her husband act so undignified. King David was dancing and rejoicing in the Lord because the ark had returned to the city. The ark's return meant God's blessing for them.

Paul said, "For I am not ashamed of the gospel of Christ: for it is the power of God unto salvation to [everyone] that [believes]; to the Jew first, and also to the Greek [non-Jews]" (Romans 1:16 KJV). Jesus said that when someone proclaims him in public, he will let the Father know that that person belongs to him. But if they deny him before others, he will tell the Father about that, too. (See Matthew 10:32-33.)

Prayer: Lord, help us to not be ashamed to rejoice and give thanks to you in front of others. Amen

Day 41

"King Xerxes commanded Queen Vashti to be brought before him, but she would not come" (Esther 1:17 NIV).

"Come to me, all you who are weary and burdened, and I will give you rest …. for your souls" (Matthew 11:28-29 NIV).

The parable of the wedding banquet in Matthew 22 is repeated in Luke 14:16-24, but it is slightly different: A man made a great feast and sent his servant to invite people to come. The servant did this but the guests one after another made excuses. One had bought property and needed to go see it. Another had bought oxen and needed to try them out. Another said he had just gotten married and couldn't come.

The man who planned the feast got angry because they refused his invitation. He told the servant to go out again and invite anyone he could find, even the poor, the blind and the lame. (These people didn't usually get invitations to the feasts of the rich.) After these people arrived there was still room, so the servant was sent out again along the highways to urge people to come. The man wanted a full house. He said to himself, "None of those who were first invited will get a crumb of my good dinner."

Prayer: Jesus, you still call, "Come to me." Help us to respond to you each day with a yes! Amen

Day 42

"This very day the Persian and Median women of the nobility who have heard about the queen's conduct will respond to all the king's nobles in the same way" (Esther 1:18 NIV).

"All we like sheep have gone astray; we have turned every one to his own way" (Isaiah 53:6 KJV).

All of us, like the queen, have responded in the same way; we have chosen to do our own thing. We like to be in charge of our lives, make our own plans and pursue our own interests. We want to enjoy the pleasures and comforts of this life. We want to chart our own course, but we aren't able to do the right thing in the right way with any consistency.

We sheep need God's help desperately.

S- Salvation	Acts 4:12
H- Healing	Luke 9:11
E- Endurance	2 Timothy 2:3
E- Encouragement	Romans 15:4
P- Peace	John 14:27

Prayer: Jesus, we all have gone astray. Good Shepherd, lead us back into the fold. Amen

Day 43

"There will be no end of disrespect and discord" (Esther 1:18 NIV).

"Wickedness [proceeds] from the wicked" (1 Samuel 24:13 KJV).

When Adam and Eve disobeyed God, sin entered the world. Since then there has been disrespect, discord and every kind of evil.

"And God saw that the wickedness of man was great in the earth, and that every imagination of the thoughts of his heart was only evil continually" (Genesis 6:5 KJV).

There will be no end to the evil; it will only get worse until Christ returns and sets up his kingdom. There will be no lasting peace until the Prince of Peace arrives on the scene.

"The kingdoms of this world are become the kingdoms of our Lord, and of his Christ; and he shall reign for ever and ever" (Revelation 11:15 KJV).

Prayer: Father, keep us from being stained by the evil in this world and help us to live holy lives. Amen

Day 44

"Therefore, if it pleases the king, let him issue a royal decree and let it be written in the laws of Persia and Media, which cannot be repealed, *that Vashti is never again to enter the presence of King Xerxes*" (Esther 1:19 NIV).

"The LORD removed them from his presence" (2 Kings 17:23 NIV).

After they sinned, Adam and Eve were kicked out of the garden and the Lord put an angel with a flaming sword to keep them away from the tree of life. He covered their sin, as shown by the animal-skin clothes he made for them, but things would never be the same. They would have to work hard now to survive and so would all those who came after them.

Since then, God has wanted a people who would love and serve him. He promises good things to those who follow his ways. But those who reject and disobey God will one day be excluded from his presence for eternity. (See 2 Thessalonians 1:8, 9.)

Queen Vashti is expelled from the king's presence; Eve is banished from the Garden; and unrepentant mankind is cast out forever. In the parable of the wedding banquet, the king noticed someone without proper wedding clothes, and he was thrown outside into the darkness. The proper wedding attire is Christ. (See Galatians 3:27.)

Prayer: Lord, clothe us with yourself. Amen

Day 45

"Also let the king give her royal position to someone else who is better than she" (Esther 1:19 NIV).

"To the one who is victorious, I will give the right to sit with me on my throne" (Revelation 3:21 NIV).

We need to be "doers of the word, and not hearers only" (James 1:22 KJV). God's word can only be effective in our lives if we heed its wisdom.

Jesus tells the church of Ephesus that they need to repent or their position will be removed. Why? Because Christ is no longer the most important love of their lives. (See Revelation 2:4-5.) All these scriptures point to the fact that we must have a fervent love for God and obey his commands to be accepted into the kingdom of God. Those who are lukewarm will be spit out of his mouth. (See Revelation 3:15-16.)

In the parable of the king and the banquet, the king sent the servants out to look for others who would come; he said the invited guests that refused to come didn't deserve the feast. Their seats were given to others. (See Matthew 22:8-10.)

Prayer: O God, keep us fervently loving and obeying you. Amen

Day 46

"Then when the king's edict is proclaimed throughout all his vast realm" (Esther 1:20 NIV).

"And this gospel of the kingdom shall be preached in all the world for a witness unto all nations; and then shall the end come" (Matthew 24:14 KJV).

The disciples had asked Jesus what would happen at the end of the world, when he returned. Jesus told them to be alert so that they would not be deceived by false prophets that would arise and even perform miracles. He told them not to be upset when there are wars and famines and earthquakes. There will be an increase of wickedness, and many will leave the faith. The gospel will be preached everywhere. In all nations there will be persecution and hatred against Christians.

If someone says that Christ has come and is in a certain place, don't believe them. Christ will come back on a cloud from heaven and everyone will see him. He will tell his angels to gather up the people who are his followers and they will be with him forever.

No one knows when his return will be, neither the angels nor the Son. Only God the Father knows and he will decide when that day will be. (See Matthew 24.)

Prayer: Lord, may we live in a state of readiness for your return. Amen

Day 47

"All the women will respect their husbands, from the least to the greatest" (Esther 1:20 NIV).

Ephesians 5:33 (NIV): "However, each one of you [husbands] also must love his wife as he loves himself, and the wife must respect her husband." "Husbands, love your wives, even as Christ also loved the church, and gave himself for it" (Ephesians 5:25 KJV).

In Genesis 2:24, the institution of marriage was established: A man was to leave his parents and be joined to his wife as one flesh. God uses the marriage relationship as a model for the mystery of Christ and the church, his bride. (See Ephesians 5:32.)

"He that is joined unto the Lord is one spirit" (1 Corinthians 6:17 KJV).

"For your Maker is your husband" (Isaiah 54:5 NIV).

We as the bride, are to respect our husband, Christ.

Prayer: Lord, prepare your church to be your bride. Amen

Day 48

"And the saying pleased the king and the princes; and the king did according to the word of Memucan" (Esther 1:21 KJV).

"And the thing pleased the king and all the congregation" (2 Chronicles 30:4 KJV).

Once king Hezekiah began to reign, he proceeded to right the wrongs of the former king, Ahaz, his father. Hezekiah had the temple reopened and all the sacred articles restored to their function. The priests were consecrated and offered sacrifices on the altar to atone for the sins of the people as the Lord required. Afterwards, the people brought thank offerings to the Lord and praised God for all he had done. Then the king and his leaders in Jerusalem had an idea to celebrate the Passover even though it was a little late. And this is what pleased the king and the congregation. (See 2 Chronicles 28-30.)

When we come to Christ, he proceeds to right the wrongs of our former king, the devil. Our "temple" is opened and sacred objects (the Holy Spirit) are restored to their intended function, which is the worship of God. Christ is the sacrifice offered to cover our sins. Then we offer thanks to the Lord and praise him for all that he has done for us.

Prayer: Lord, you have restored our temple. May we worship you. Amen

Day 49

"He sent dispatches to all parts of the kingdom, to each province in its own script and to each people in their own language ... using his native tongue" (Esther 1:22 NIV).

"The LORD ... [confounded] the language of all the earth" (Genesis 11:9 KJV).

This is the first reference in Esther to the different languages of the kingdom.

We know from Genesis 11:1-9, that the world once had one language and the people had settled together. They made bricks and built a city so they wouldn't be scattered all over the place. This went directly against God's command for them to occupy all the earth. Also, they planned to make a tower that would be so tall it would make them famous.

The Lord decided to come down from heaven and look over this city and tower. What he saw was that these people all speaking one language could collectively come up with any idea and pursue it and that would be disastrous. So the Lord gave them different languages. Each language group went off to live in an area of their own. They called the place Babel. This is how the Lord had them separate and fill the earth with people.

Prayer: Lord, use us to build your Kingdom, not our own. Amen

"Proclaiming that every man should be ruler over his own household" (Esther 1:22 NIV).

"But I would have you know, that the head of every man is Christ; and the head of the woman is the man" (1 Corinthians 11:3 KJV). "Wives, submit yourselves unto your own husbands, as it is fit in the Lord. Husbands, love your wives, and be not bitter against them. Children, obey your parents in all things: for this is well pleasing unto the Lord" (Colossians 3:18-20 KJV).

Christ, as our husband, is to be ruler over his household, the church. We have the Bible as our guide. He is to be the authority figure and director for the church. We are to submit to him above any church authorities and all decisions should be made with his will and purposes in mind.

In the verses above we see God's established authority in its smallest, most vulnerable place, the home. The family is a micro-society and when it starts to crumble the society-at-large begins to crumble. The devil knows this so he makes the family his number-one target.

Prayer: Father, there is a massive attack from the enemy on the family; please preserve the family unit as you laid out in your Word. Amen

Day 51

Chapter 1 Review

Day 6: God is Father, Son, and Holy Spirit.

Day 15: We can have a personal relationship with the Creator.

Day 25: We are not to put restrictions on others and judge them. God will take care of them.

Day 27: This is how sin entered the world: Adam and Eve chose to decide for themselves what was right and wrong instead of trusting God's wisdom and limits.

Day 28: Christ paid for the sins of all people on the cross.

Day 30: God the Father welcomes home the repentant sinner.

Day 31: Sins can be forgiven but there are still consequences.

Day 33: God continues to call lost people, but many, like Queen Vashti, refuse to come.

Day 43: There will be no lasting peace until the Prince of Peace arrives.

Day 47: God uses the marriage relationship as a model for the mystery of Christ and the church, his Bride.

Prayer: Lord, you have done so much for us. May we give our all to you. Amen

Chapter 1 Challenge

Answer the questions below.

1. Who ruled over 127 provinces? (1:1)

2. Where was his royal throne? (1:2)

3. In what year of his reign did he give a banquet for all his nobles? (1:3)

4. He gave another banquet right after that. Who was it for? (1:5)

5. What drink was served at the banquet? (1:7)

6. Who gave a banquet for the women in the royal palace? (1:9)

7. The king commanded that the queen be brought for what purpose? (1:11)

8. How did she respond? And how did the king feel about her response? (1:12)

9. What were the consequences of her decision? Name three. (1:16-19)

Prayer: Lord, teach us from your Word how we can please you. Amen

Day 53

"Later when King Xerxes' fury had subsided, *he remembered Vashti* and what she had done and what he had decreed about her" (Esther 2:1 NIV).

"God remembered Noah" (Genesis 8:1 KJV).

God "did not spare the ancient world when he brought the flood on its ungodly people, but protected Noah, a preacher of righteousness, and seven others" (2 Peter 2:5 NIV). People's wickedness moved God to wipe out the inhabitants of the earth by a flood; but righteous Noah and his family and the animals in the ark were spared. (See Genesis 6-8 for the story of Noah and the Ark.)

Just as God had Noah prepare the ark for his safety during the flood, God sent his Son Jesus as our ark of safety. Noah is a type of Jesus who rescues the "seven"—the complete world. With Christ we are safe from the flood of evil in this world. The ark of Christ will carry us to the Father and we will live with Him forever!

Prayer: Father, thank you for sending Jesus to rescue us from the flood. Amen

"Then the king's personal attendants proposed, *'Let a search be made'*" (Esther 2:2 NIV).

"I, even I, will both search [for] my sheep, and seek them out" (Ezekiel 34:11 KJV).

God often refers to his people as sheep. Sheep aren't the most intelligent animals and they are high maintenance—that's why they need a shepherd.

Jesus said, "I am the good shepherd, and know my sheep. ... I lay down my life for the sheep" (John 10:14-15 KJV). Jesus told his disciples that a hired hand who doesn't own the sheep will run away when a wolf comes because he doesn't care about the sheep. But Jesus is the good shepherd he knows his sheep and cares for them—even to the point of dying for them. The sheep know their shepherd's voice and they follow him; but a stranger's voice they won't follow.

Jesus came searching for us to save us. "The Son of man is not come to destroy men's lives, but to save them" (Luke 9:56 KJV). (God wants to save us—more than we want to be saved.)

Prayer: Father, thank you for being patient with us sheep. Amen

Day 55

"For beautiful young virgins for the king" (Esther 2:2 NIV).

"Remember your Creator in the days of your youth" (Ecclesiastes 12:1 NIV).

Turn to God while you are young; don't put it off.

Don't let people discourage you—follow God and be a good example to others by your love, faith and clean living. How can you live a clean life? By using the Bible as the instruction manual for your daily choices. Know what God says about an issue—then take it to heart. His Word will light the way for you to walk. (See 1 Timothy 4:12; Psalm 119:9-11, 105.)

God gave four young Israelite men special knowledge and understanding in their studies in Babylon. The king was so impressed by them; they were chosen to serve him. One was especially gifted in understanding visions and interpreting dreams. His name was Daniel. (See Daniel 1.)

Let's pray that God raises up young men and women to serve the King.

Prayer: Lord, remind us to consult your Word so we can make choices that please you. Amen

"Let the king appoint commissioners in every province of his realm" (Esther 2:3 NIV).

"He appointed twelve … that he might send them out to preach" (Mark 3:14 NIV).

The twelve disciples Jesus called to follow him were James and his brother, John; Simon (Peter) and his brother Andrew (these four were fishermen by trade); Philip, Bartholomew, Thomas and Matthew the tax collector; also, James, Thaddaeus, Simon the Zealot and Judas Iscariot, who later betrayed Jesus. These twelve traveled around with Jesus and were his closest disciples. He sent them out to preach and gave them authority to do mighty works in his name.

In the parable of the wedding banquet (Matthew 22) the king repeatedly sent his servants out to bring as many as would come to his banquet.

Jesus still calls disciples. He appoints and commissions them to go and spread the good news of the gospel throughout the world.

Prayer: Lord, as you send us out, go with us and speak through us. Amen

Day 57

"To bring all these beautiful young women into the harem at the citadel of Susa" (Esther 2:3 NIV).

God is patient. He doesn't want anyone to perish; he wants everyone to turn from their sins and receive his love and forgiveness. (See 2 Peter 3:9.)

Susa represents heaven. God wants all brought to him in heaven.

Cornelius was a Gentile (non-Jew) who feared God. An angel had visited him and told him to have Peter come. When Peter arrived; he preached about Jesus and the Holy Spirit fell on those in the room. The men with Peter were astonished that the Gentiles received the Holy Spirit. (The Jews thought that salvation was only for them.) Peter realized that God's gift of salvation and his Spirit were meant for all races and nations. (See Acts 10.)

In the parable of the wedding banquet, at the king's command "those servants went out … and gathered together … both bad and good: and the wedding was furnished with guests" (Matthew 22:10 KJV).

Prayer: Thank you, Lord, that your salvation is for all. Amen

"Let them be placed under the care of Hegai" (Esther 2:3 NIV).

God's Spirit "shall teach you all things" (John 14:26 KJV).

Hegai, and all the eunuchs represent the Holy Spirit. We are placed under the care of the Holy Spirit.

We are all broken and need some TLC. Jesus knows we can't make it on our own. He was going to leave this world so he was giving words of encouragement to his disciples—the disciples of that day and the disciples of the future. Jesus said, "I will pray [to] the Father, and he shall give you another Comforter, that he may abide with you for ever" (John 14:16 KJV).

Jesus did not leave us without help. He sent the Spirit to lead, guide and direct us; to be with us and in us. The Holy Spirit will remind us of what Jesus has said to us—his commands and promises. He will teach us how to be royalty. We once were commoners but now we are royalty; we have been chosen by the King.

Prayer: Lord, remind us who we are in you, a child of the King. Amen

Day 59

"The king's eunuch, who is in charge of the women" (Esther 2:3 NIV).

"Walk not after the flesh, but after the Spirit" (Romans 8:1 KJV).

Once we have given our hearts to Jesus; we are to give him our lives also. Once "we" were in charge of our lives; now the Holy Spirit is to be in charge. Christ's death and resurrection has made it possible for us to be set free from sin and death.

Now because of Christ we can live lives pleasing to God if we listen to the Spirit's promptings. Those who are lost (without Christ) live their lives by their natural desires; but if those who are in Christ live by the Spirit's direction, they have life and peace. People who are controlled by their sinful, natural desires aren't pleasing God.

If God's Spirit lives in you and you yield to him you are truly a disciple of Christ. The same Spirit that gave life to Jesus and raised him up from death, gives life to our bodies.

In Christ, we have the responsibility of living lives that please him. If we continue to live according to our sinful nature we will die spiritually. But if we kill off all the wicked deeds of our flesh we will live—eternally. Those who give the Holy Spirit charge of their lives are God's children. (See Romans 8:1-14.)

Prayer: Lord, help us to yield to your Holy Spirit. Amen

"And let beauty treatments be given to them" (Esther 2:3 NIV).

"To bestow on them a crown of beauty" (Isaiah 61:3 NIV).

The beauty treatments are given to us from God. We can't make our own selves beautiful inside. If we try to clean up ourselves it's like washing with a dirty washcloth; we just spread the filth around. (See Isaiah 64:6.) He makes us beautiful by washing us clean with the word of God. Being in God's word and obeying his Word changes us. (See Ephesians 5:26.)

The Lord asked the prophet Jeremiah, "Is not my word like as a fire? ... and like a hammer that [breaks] the rock in pieces?" (Jeremiah 23:29 KJV). Ouch. This is how the Lord makes his people beautiful; by burning up the garbage in us and breaking to pieces our selfish stubbornness.

The Holy Spirit is making the church beautiful to God; not necessarily beautiful in others' eyes. People judge us by our appearance, but God looks at our hearts. (See 1 Samuel 16:7.)

Prayer: Thank you God, that you are making us beautiful. Amen

Day 61

"Then let the young woman who pleases the king be queen instead of Vashti" (Esther 2:4 NIV).

"But without faith it is impossible to please him" (Hebrews 11:6 KJV).

We please God by walking in faith and obedience to his will. Everything we obtain from God is by faith—even the faith to believe he exists. Faith itself comes from God—he gives each of us a portion—and that faith grows as we trust in him. It's by faith we believe that he rewards those who follow him. (See Romans 12:3; Hebrews 11:6.)

Hearing and reading about God from the Bible is good, but we must go a step further and actually do what it says. It's not those who claim to be a Christian who will make it to heaven, but those who do God's will and not their own. (See Matthew 7:21.)

Those who live their lives to please the King of kings will be chosen as his Bride.

Prayer: Father, help us to walk in faith so that our lives will be pleasing to you. Amen

"This advice appealed to the king, and he followed it" (Esther 2:4 NIV).

"The wise listen to advice" (Proverbs 12:15 NIV).

We can give God advice on how to answer our prayers and he may choose to do it that way, or not; and most likely not. The Lord says, "My thoughts are not your thoughts, neither are your ways my ways" (Isaiah 55:8 KJV). He is wiser than we are, and he knows our problems better than we do. So let's put them in his hands and let him work things out in his way and time.

Our prayers for others and for ourselves are often a request that God spare us and them from hardship and pain. But in this world we will encounter trials. These trials and troubles test our faith and make it stronger. When Jesus prayed to the Father for his disciples; he prayed that God would not take them out of the world but keep them from the evil in it. He didn't pray for them to have a pain-free life. (See John 17:11, 15.)

Prayer: Lord, help us to trust you in the difficult times of life because you know what is best for us. Amen

Day 63

"*Now there was in the citadel of Susa a Jew of the tribe of Benjamin, named Mordecai son of Jair, the son of Shimei, the son of Kish*" (Esther 2:5 NIV).

This is "where Christ is, seated at the right hand of God" (Colossians 3:1 NIV).

Susa represents heaven. Jesus, was born a Jew (his mother was Jewish). Benjamin means "son of the right hand." Mordecai represents Jesus Christ, the Son, who is now sitting at God's right hand in heaven.

We have the expression that a certain person is my "right-hand" or "right-hand man" for someone who is always there to help us. Jesus was God's right-hand man. He did whatever the Father needed him to do.

David said the Lord was at his right hand. The Lord gave him counsel and direction for his life and helped him stay steady during difficult times. (See Psalm 16.)

In Isaiah 41:13, the Lord says he will hold our right hand and we are not to be afraid because he will help us.

Prayer: Lord, keep hold of our hands today. Amen

"Who had been carried into exile from Jerusalem by Nebuchadnezzar *king* of Babylon" (Esther 2:6 NIV).

Jesus said, "I have not come on my own; God sent me" (John 8:42 NIV).

Mordecai had been carried into exile by the king of Babylon; this represents Jesus being sent from heaven by God; he didn't come on his own. But Jesus willingly left heaven, put on an earthly body and lived among us. He was sent because of the love of the Father for us. He lived here for a time and accomplished the will of the Father by dying for the sins of the people of the whole world. He rose from the dead and is once again with God the Father. (See John 1:14; 3:16.)

God told Abram (Abraham) to leave his country and relatives and go to a different land. Because of his faith in God, he obeyed. He packed up and left not knowing where he was going. God led him to what would be the future land of the Israelites—what was later called the Promised Land. (See Genesis 12:1; Hebrews 11:8-9.)

Prayer: Lord, help us to step out in faith and obey when you call us to leave the familiar and go to into a situation or place that is a "foreign country" to us. Amen

Day 65

"Among those taken captive with Jehoiachin king of Judah" (Esther 2:6 NIV).

We are to be "bringing into captivity every thought to the obedience of Christ" (2 Corinthians 10:5 KJV).

We are to take our thoughts captive—to have them under control, by the help of the Holy Spirit. Our thoughts find expression in our words, emotions and actions. Changing the way we think changes the way we talk, feel and act; it changes our lives.

As we immerse ourselves in God's word—the truth—we can better recognize the lies the enemy tells us and dismiss them from our thoughts. Memorizing scripture is a big help in having the truth handy so we won't be tripped up by the devil's accusing voice. (See Psalm 119:11.)

Here are two scriptures we can pray to the Lord concerning our thoughts:

"Search me, O God, and know my heart: try me, and know my thoughts: And see if there be any wicked way in me, and lead me in the way everlasting" (Psalm 139:23-24 KJV).

"Let the words of my mouth, and the meditation of my heart, be acceptable in [your] sight, O LORD, my strength, and my redeemer" (Psalm 19:14 KJV).

Prayer: Lord, help our thoughts to be pleasing to you. Amen

Day 66

"Mordecai had a cousin named Hadassah, *whom he had brought up*" (Esther 2:7 NIV).

He wants us to "grow up into him in all things" (Ephesians 4:15 KJV).

God does not want us to stay baby Christians, but to grow up. Growing up is a long, slow process, but God is very patient. He takes us as we are, but then he starts the process of "bringing us up" into maturity.

As we grow up in him, he produces in us the fruit of the Spirit which is love, joy, peace, patience, gentleness, goodness, faith, humility and self-control. Jesus said we need to stay close to him for without his help we can't produce this good fruit. (See 1 Corinthians 3:1-3; Galatians 5:22-23; John 15:4-5.)

> Grow up means to slow up. (Take the time to do a good job.)
>
> Grow up means to show up. (Be there—be responsible.)
>
> Grow up means to listen up. (Hear the other person's view.)
>
> Grow up means to wise up. (Obey the Lord.)

Prayer: Father, as we grow up in you, may the fruit of the Spirit be evident in our lives. Amen

Day 67

"Because she had neither father nor mother" (Esther 2:7 NIV).

"When my father and my mother forsake me, then the Lord will take me up" (Psalm 27:10 KJV).

The time comes when we no longer have our parents to care for us. As adults we begin a life of our own and learn to be more independent—physically, emotionally and even spiritually; for we can't live on the faith of our parents, friends or spouse. We must have our own personal "born again" experience. (See John 3.) But this greater independence is to be in our earthly relationships and not with our Heavenly Father. He wants us to be totally dependent on him.

God is a loving Father. "A father of the fatherless ... is God" (Psalm 68:5 KJV). He will take care of us if we put our faith and trust in him. Family and friends may leave us, but the Lord will stand with us. He won't forsake us. (See Hebrews 13:5.)

Prayer: Heavenly Father, we depend on you, thank you that you take care of us. Amen

"This young woman, who was also known as Esther, had a lovely figure and was beautiful" (Esther 2:7 NIV).

"How beautiful you are, my darling! Oh, how beautiful!" (Song of Songs 1:15 NIV).

Esther represents the bride of Christ and she is beautiful. We aren't talking about outward beauty that comes from: a pretty face, expensive jewelry, fancy hairdos and stylish clothes; we are talking about inner beauty of the heart, a submissive and gentle spirit, which is important to God. (See 1 Peter 3:3-4.)

The world gives attention and favor to those with outward, physical beauty. God looks on the heart and is pleased with the inner beauty of love and kindness. God's beauty queens look different from the world's beauty queens.

Prayer: Thank you, God, that we don't have to compete with anyone. You think we are beautiful and that is what really matters. Amen

Day 69

"Mordecai had taken her as his own daughter when her father and mother died" (Esther 2:7 NIV).

"I will be a Father to you, and you will be my sons and daughters" (2 Corinthians 6:18 NIV).

Here are some verses that talk about us being God's children.

"But as many as received him, to them gave he power to become the sons of God, even to them that believe on his name" (John 1:12 KJV).

"For [you] are all the children of God by faith in Christ Jesus" (Galatians 3:26 KJV).

"And if children, then heirs; heirs of God, and joint-heirs with Christ; if so be that we suffer with him, that we may be also glorified together" (Romans 8:17 KJV).

The Father greatly loves us and calls us his children. "Now are we the sons [and daughters] of God, and it [does] not yet appear what we shall be: but we know that, when he shall appear, we shall be like him; for we shall see him as he is." And we that have this hope in him strive to live a pure life, because he is pure. We can tell who the children of God are and who the devil's children are. God's children do what is right and they love their brothers and sisters. (See 1 John 3:1-3, 10. v. 2 KJV.)

Prayer: Father, thank you that we are your children. Amen

"When the king's order and edict had been proclaimed, *many young women were brought to the citadel of Susa and put under the care of Hegai. Esther also was taken to the king's palace and entrusted to Hegai, who had charge of the harem*" (Esther 2:8 NIV).

"If we live in the Spirit, let us also walk in the Spirit" (Galatians 5:25 KJV).

Esther (Christ's bride-to-be) is put under the care of Hegai (the Holy Spirit).

We need the guidance of the Spirit because we have three major areas to combat in the Christian life: the world, the flesh, and the devil.

The world. The world refers to the lost—those who don't follow Jesus Christ. They don't adhere to the teachings of the Bible, but have their own standards of right and wrong. They can influence Christians, so we must be alert to this.

The flesh. Our sinful nature, or our flesh, is at odds with the Spirit of God in us. We want God to miraculously change us, but change is a day-by-day lifetime endeavor.

The devil. A fallen angel who deceives the world and accuses the believers. He wreaks havoc in the world and opposes the work of God in people's lives.

Prayer: God, help us yield to the leading of the Spirit so we will not be swayed by the world, the flesh and the devil. Amen

Day 71

"She pleased him and won *his favor*" (Esther 2:9 NIV).

"I tell you, now is the time of God's favor, now is the day of salvation" (2 Corinthians 6:2 NIV).

Jesus told a parable of a rich man whose field produced a great harvest. The man didn't know where to store all his crops. Then he had the idea to tear down his old storage building and build new and bigger ones. Since he had so much, he figured he would retire and live the easy life from now on. But God called him a fool and said his time was up. This is what happens to those who hoard earthly things instead of being generous in giving to God and his kingdom. (See Luke 12:16-21.)

We are not promised tomorrow. Today is the day to connect with God. Now is the time to live in God's favor. Someday the opportunity will be over and we will be sorry if we miss it.

Prayer: Lord, may we not be caught up with the things of this world but be living for your kingdom. Amen

"Immediately he provided her with her beauty treatments" (Esther 2:9 NIV).

"If we confess our sins, he is faithful and just to forgive us our sins, and to cleanse us from all unrighteousness" (1 John 1:9 KJV).

If we are sorry for our sins and ask God for his forgiveness, immediately we are made clean and beautiful in his sight. God provides all that we need to make us beautiful to him.

> "Worship the LORD in the beauty of holiness."
> "And let the beauty of the LORD our God be upon us."
> "He will beautify the meek with salvation."
> (Psalm 29:2, 90:17, 149:4 KJV)

> God is the one who makes us beautiful. He is beautiful and he imparts that beauty of holiness and salvation in his church. This is inward beauty because "[favor] is deceitful, and [outward] beauty is vain: but a woman that [fears] the LORD, she shall be praised" (Proverbs 31:30 KJV).

Prayer: Lord, you are beautiful and your touch makes us beautiful. Amen

Day 73

"And special food" (Esther 2:9 NIV).

"He shall ... eat of the holy things; because it is his food" (Leviticus 22:7 KJV).

Earthly food isn't enough; we need God's word to sustain us. (See Matthew 4:4.) Jesus said that his food was to do his Father's will. (See John 4:34). May doing the Father's will be the food that keeps us going—giving us hope and purpose for our lives.

Our physical appetite for food can sometimes be our undoing. Here are a few of the incidents in the Bible concerning food and how it caused them trouble:

Adam and Eve ate from the tree they were not supposed to and sin entered the world.

Esau sold his birthright to his brother Jacob for a bowl of stew and was later very sorry.

The Israelites complained to the Lord that they didn't have meat. So he sent them quail but while it was still in their mouths, he struck them with a plague.

Paul spoke of those whose god was their belly.

Jesus asked the crowd if there wasn't more to life than just eating.

(See Genesis 3:6, 25:29-34; Numbers 11:31-33; 1 Kings 13, Philippians 3:19; Matthew 6:25.)

Prayer: God, help us to keep our fleshly appetites under control by the help of your Holy Spirit. Amen

"He assigned to her seven female attendants selected from the king's palace" (Esther 2:9 NIV).

"His divine power has given us everything we need for a godly life" (2 Peter 1:3 NIV).

Esther didn't choose the attendants herself; the king assigned them to her.

The Lord provides all that we need to live a godly life and to know him. He also gives us "great and precious promises: that by these [we] might be partakers of the divine nature, having escaped the corruption that is in the world" (2 Peter 1:4 KJV). Again, we have the number seven meaning complete; he makes available <u>all</u> we need to live a life pleasing to him. It is up to us to use what he has already provided.

Our King assigns to his church seven attendants or helpers to prepare her for her future position as the bride of Christ. We don't choose these for ourselves; they are the helpers we need (but don't want). The seven attendants are: trouble, sorrow, temptation, suffering, the poor, persecution and death. We will explore each of these in the following week.

Prayer: Thank you, God, that you provide all we need to live for you. Amen

Day 75

"I have told you these things, so that in me you may have peace. In this world you will have trouble. But take heart! I have overcome the world" (John 16:33 NIV).

1. Trouble: Jesus said we would have trouble in this world, but he also promised we would have peace in him. Keeping our minds on Christ and his promises increases our trust in him and produces peace in our hearts even in midst of trouble. (See Isaiah 26:3.)

   Sometimes trouble is of our own making: we made a poor choice and now we are paying for it. Even then, the Lord can use it for his glory if we surrender it to him and follow his guidance in how to best untangle the mess we have made. Sometimes that means to do nothing except pray and wait on him to work it out.

   When the trouble is not of our doing and out of our control to fix, we still need his help in having the right attitude and patience, so we don't get bitter or angry over it. Praying that his will be done in the situation is the right way to go.

Prayer: Lord, be with us in trouble and bring us out, for your glory. Amen

"Blessed are they that mourn: for they shall be comforted" (Matthew 5:4 KJV).

2. Sorrow: God is with us in our sorrow and he brings comfort. This is a prophecy about Jesus: "He is despised and rejected of men; a man of sorrows, and acquainted with grief" and it goes on to say he has "carried our sorrows" (Isaiah 53:3-4 KJV). Jesus suffered grief and sorrow when he was here in this world. He understands what it feels like, so we can go to him with ours and ask for his comfort.

   In John 11, Jesus wept with Mary and Martha at the grave of Lazarus. He was not weeping for the loss of Lazarus, because he had already planned to raise him from the dead. He was weeping because of the sorrow of Mary and Martha; they were his friends. He was joining in their sorrow and grief as a way of comforting them. Their sorrow was turned to joy when he raised up Lazarus.

Prayer: Lord, please comfort those who are sorrowing today. Amen

Day 77

"Each person is tempted" (James 1:14 NIV).

3. Temptation: God doesn't tempt us. (See James 1:13.) But he does allow us to be tempted. Jesus was tempted but didn't sin. He is willing to help us in our temptation. (See Hebrews 2:18.) There is not a temptation that comes to us as children of God that we can't resist if we rely on his power; he will show us the way through it.

    "No temptation has overtaken you except what is common to mankind. And God is faithful; he will not let you be tempted beyond what you can bear. But when you are tempted, he will also provide a way out so that you can endure it" (1 Corinthians 10:13 NIV).

    When we are tempted, will we choose our way or God's way? Pray and ask for strength from Jesus who "is able to keep you from falling" (Jude 1:24 KJV). He has a perfect track record.

Prayer: Lord, when we are tempted give us the strength and the will to choose your way. Amen

"Though he were a Son, yet [he] learned ... obedience by the things which he suffered" (Hebrews 5:8 KJV).

4. Suffering: Suffering is part of the program; Jesus wasn't spared it and neither are we. Just as Christ suffered in his human body by doing God's will, we will suffer also. When we refuse to pamper this flesh of ours and resist sin in order to do the will of God, we will experience suffering and pain. But it is better to suffer for doing good than for doing wrong. (See 1 Peter 3:17, 4:1-2.)

    Parents discipline their children because they love them and want them to grow up doing what is right. God disciplines his children because he loves us and wants us to be holy. Submitting to his authority is painful, but it produces the fruit of the Spirit in us. (See Hebrews 12:5-11.)

    Of course, there is also suffering that occurs just because we live on this planet Earth where sin introduced all kinds of suffering, pain and death. We need his grace and help just as much in those situations.

Prayer: Lord, help us in our suffering to be faithful to you. Amen

Day 79

"Whoever is kind to the poor lends to the LORD, and he will reward them for what they have done" (Proverbs 19:17 NIV).

5. The poor: God cares about the poor and so should we. God will bless those who help the needy. The poor and needy might not be just those who live on the streets. They could be those in your neighborhood or in your church who could use a helping hand. The needy person could be someone in your own family and you are the caregiver.

   We can all help someone, even if our resources are limited. Giving to food pantries, homeless shelters and providing meals for the poor are some things we could be involved in. Calling or visiting those who are in nursing homes or confined to their homes can be a blessing to them and to us. Jesus said there would always be poor people, so there is always a ministry for us—to help them. (See Mark 14:7.)

Prayer: Lord, open our eyes to the needs around us and help us to meet them, in your name. Amen

Day 80

"All that will live godly in Christ Jesus shall suffer persecution" (2 Timothy 3:12 KJV).

6. Persecution: Jesus warned his disciples that they would have enemies and would be persecuted. He told them to "love your enemies, bless them that curse you, do good to them that hate you, and pray for them which despitefully use you, and persecute you" (Matthew 5:44 KJV). Those who live godly lives will stand out among others as being different. This can cause tension and conflict, as it did with Jesus.

   There are stories in the Bible from the beginning to the end that tell of the righteous being persecuted, even killed. Cain killed his brother, Abel. (Genesis 4) Joseph's brothers sold him. (Genesis 37) The Israelites killed the prophets the Lord sent them. (Nehemiah 9:26) John the Baptist was beheaded. (Matthew 14) Jesus was crucified. (John 19) Stephen was stoned. (Acts 7) James was killed with a sword. (Acts 12:2) Paul was imprisoned and later killed. (2 Corinthians 11:23-27) Those who didn't worship the beast were beheaded. (Revelation 20:4)

Prayer: Lord, help us to stand up for the right even if it causes us to be persecuted. Amen

Day 81

"For this God is our God for ever and ever: he will be our guide even unto death" (Psalm 48:14 KJV).

7. Death: Death is something we all must face unless the Lord returns first. If we are in Christ, we need not fear death. Jesus has gone before us and conquered death.

    "So when this corruptible shall have put on incorruption, and this mortal [body] shall have put on immortality, then shall be brought to pass the saying that is written, Death is swallowed up in victory. O death, where is [your] sting? O grave, where is [your] victory? But thanks be to God, which [gives] us the victory through our Lord Jesus Christ" (1 Corinthians 15:54-55, 57 KJV).

    For the believer "to be absent from the body [is] to be present with the Lord" (2 Corinthians 5:8 KJV). The death of our physical body is not the end of us. We live on in eternity with God—or without him. "Precious in the sight of the LORD is the death of his saints" (Psalm 116:15 KJV). If we can trust God with our life, let us trust him to be with us in our death.

Prayer: Lord, let us trust you in life and in death. Amen

Esther Chapter 2

Day 82

"And moved her and her attendants into the best place in the harem" (Esther 2:9 NIV).

"No good thing will he withhold from them that walk uprightly" (Psalm 84:11 KJV).

God moves us and our "attendants" (our circumstances of trouble, sorrow or temptation) so that we are in the best place for him to make us into the spotless bride he desires, a bride conformed to the image of his Son. "For whom he did foreknow, he also did predestinate to be conformed to the image of his Son" (Romans 8:29 KJV). Christ gave his life for the church "that he might present it to himself a glorious church, not having spot, or wrinkle, or any such thing; but that it should be holy and without blemish" (Ephesians 5:27 KJV).

The Bride is to be a helper and companion for his Son. God moves us to the "best place" even though it may not look good or feel comfortable. These attendants will be with us all of our days. There will never be a time we can say we have arrived at perfection, not on this earth. We daily need God's help and grace to stay on "the straight and narrow."

Prayer: Father, keep us close to you. Amen

Day 83

"Esther had not revealed her nationality and family background, because Mordecai had forbidden her to do so" (Esther 2:10 NIV).

"God is no respecter of persons: But in every nation he that [fears] him, and [works] righteousness, is accepted with him" (Acts 10:34-35 KJV).

Our nationality and family background don't matter to God; his salvation is for all. God accepts us as we are when we come to him.

Think of God's family as a tree. Some Jewish branches were broken off because of their unbelief. God in his mercy grafted in other branches, the Gentiles, when they believed in his Son. But Gentiles, don't get proud: you only are in the tree by faith. Lose that and you will be broken off as well. And if the Jews come to believe in Christ, they will be grafted back into God's tree. (See Romans 11:17-24.)

Our family history may be something we aren't proud of, but God accepts us into his family. The country we are from doesn't matter now. Like the saints of old, we have a heavenly citizenship. (See Hebrews 11:13-16.)

Prayer: Thank you, God, that you welcome anyone from any country or any background into your family when they believe in your Son. Amen

"And Mordecai walked every day before the court of the women's house, to know how Esther did, and what should become of her" (Esther 2:11 KJV).

"The eyes of the Lord are upon the righteous, and his ears are open unto their cry" (Psalm 34:15 KJV).

Just as Mordecai kept tabs on Esther every day, so the Lord keeps his eyes on us every day. The Lord is with us; he knows what is happening in our lives. He sees when we sit or stand; he knows our thoughts and knows what we are going to say before we say it. The darkness of night is not dark to him; he can see us as if it were daytime. (See Psalm 34:7, 139:1-12.) He not only sees us, but is working on our behalf so his will can be done in us. "For it is God which [works] in you both to will and to do of his good pleasure" (Philippians 2:13 KJV).

He hears and answers when we call to him. "He that planted the ear, shall he not hear? he that formed the eye, shall he not see?" (Psalm 94:9 KJV).

Prayer: Thank you, Lord, that you know us so intimately. Amen

Day 85

"Before a young woman's turn came to go in to King Xerxes" (Esther 2:12 NIV).

"Prepare to meet your God" (Amos 4:12 NIV).

These young women represent new believers in Christ. "For by grace are [you] saved through faith; and that not of yourselves; it is the gift of God: Not of works, lest any man should boast" (Ephesians 2:8-9 KJV). When we come to Christ we are washed clean, forgiven and are righteous in God's eyes and prepared to meet him.

"He [has] chosen us in him before the foundation of the world, that we should be holy and without blame before him in love." He decided beforehand to adopt us as his children through his Son, Christ Jesus "according to the good pleasure of his will .... In whom we have redemption through his blood, the forgiveness of sins, according to the riches of his grace; ... In whom also we have obtained an inheritance, ... That we should be to the praise of his glory" (Ephesians 1:4-5, 7, 11-12 KJV).

These are just a few of the awesome things we receive from the Mighty God when we commit to living for him. He loves us and wants us for himself. He desires to be with us.

Prayer: Lord, thank you for loving us and giving us so much. Amen

"She had to complete twelve months of beauty treatments prescribed for the women, six months with oil of myrrh and six with perfumes and cosmetics" (Esther 2:12 NIV).

"And the evening and the morning were the sixth day" (Genesis 1:31 KJV).

Six is symbolic of humans, who were created on day six. Because of the fall of Adam and Eve, people are sinful and unholy and need to be beautified. Twelve is the number of God's chosen ones: the twelve tribes of Israel and the twelve disciples.

Esther and these young women had to surrender their bodies to receive the beautifying process and so do we. "Present your bodies a living sacrifice, holy, acceptable unto God" (Romans 12:1 KJV). Six represents our worldliness; in Christ we are changed to a twelve, the "chosen" of God. Romans 12:2 (KJV): "And be not conformed to this world: but be … transformed by the renewing of your mind." We present ourselves to God and he transforms us by renewing our minds; this is one of the beauty treatments for Christ's bride.

Prayer: Lord, transform us by the renewing of our minds, so that we may walk as the chosen ones of God. Amen

Day 87

"With perfumes and cosmetics" (Esther 2:12 NIV).

"Then Mary took … an expensive perfume; she poured it on Jesus' feet" (John 12:3 NIV).

Jesus went to the home of Lazarus (whom he had earlier raised from the dead) where a dinner was held to honor Jesus. Martha was busy serving and Lazarus was at the table with him. Martha's sister Mary took a large amount of costly perfume and poured it on Jesus' feet and dried his feet with her hair.

Judas, the disciple who would later betray Jesus, complained to him that this perfume could have been sold, and the money given to help the poor. Judas wasn't concerned about the poor; he wanted to sell the perfume so he could take some of the money for himself. He was the treasurer for the disciples and regularly stole from the money bag. Jesus told Judas to stop bothering Mary. Jesus said there would always be poor people to help; but he would not always be there. (See John 12:1-8.)

Mary's sacrificial gift of the perfume was her act of worship to the Lord. It was her way of honoring him. She offered the best of what she had to the Lord. "She [has] done what she could" (Mark 14:8 KJV).

Prayer: Lord, help us to offer our best to you as our act of worship. Amen

"And this is how she would go to the king" (Esther 2:13 NIV).

"With gladness and rejoicing … they shall enter into the king's palace." "Come before his presence with singing. … Enter into his gates with thanksgiving, and into his courts with praise" (Psalm 45:15, 100:2, 4 KJV).

The verses above tell us how we should go to the King.

There are many references in the Bible about praising God and singing to the Lord, especially in the Psalms. As you read through the Psalms, "give thanks unto the LORD, for he is good: for his mercy [endures forever]" (Psalm 107:1 KJV).

Ephesians 5:19-20 (KJV): "Speaking to yourselves in psalms and hymns and spiritual songs, singing and making melody in your heart to the Lord: Giving thanks always for all things … in the name of our Lord Jesus Christ."

Don't worry about your singing ability; he gave you the voice you have. He would love to hear you sing to him.

"I will sing unto the Lord as long as I live: I will sing praise to my God" (Psalm 104:33 KJV).

Prayer: Lord, may we sing praises to you every day. Amen

Day 89

"Anything she wanted was given her to take with her from the harem to the king's palace" (Esther 2:13 NIV).

"Take with you words, and turn to the LORD" (Hosea 14:2 KJV).

We can take anything we want to the Lord, the good things and the bad, our doubts and our fears. "Casting all your care upon him; for he [cares] for you" (1 Peter 5:7 KJV). He hears our prayers and wants us to give him our burdens. He is full of love and compassion.

"Look upon [my] affliction and my pain" (Psalm 25:18 KJV).

There was a famine in the land and the Lord directed Elijah to a widow, whom the Lord said was to feed him. When he found her, she was gathering sticks to make a last meal for herself and her son. Elijah asked her for a piece of bread; she didn't have any. She only had a little flour and oil. Elijah told her to go and make him some bread and then make some for her and her son. He promised that the flour and oil would not run out until the Lord sent the rain to grow crops again. She did as Elijah said and she never ran out of flour and oil. She had food for herself, her family and Elijah, just as the Lord said. (See 1 Kings 17:7-16.)

She gave what little she had to the prophet, trusting in the word of the Lord to supply her needs as he promised.

Prayer: Lord, we give you our cares, please meet our needs. Amen

"In the evening she would go there and in the morning" (Esther 2:14 NIV).

"Evening, and morning, and at noon, will I pray, and cry aloud: and he shall hear my voice" (Psalm 55:17 KJV).

This symbolizes believers going into the presence of God in the evening and in the morning for prayer. Prayer is talking (and listening) to God. A relationship is maintained by communication. Evening, morning and throughout the day we can speak to our heavenly Father, silently in our hearts or out loud. He knows our thoughts and hears our words. He receives our prayers like a fragrant perfume ascending up to him:

"And I saw the seven angels which stood before God. ... And another angel came and stood at the altar, having a golden censer; and there was given unto him much incense, that he should offer it with the prayers of all saints upon the golden altar which was before the throne. And the smoke of the incense, which came with the prayers of the saints, ascended up before God" (Revelation 8:2-4 KJV).

Jesus said when we pray, we should go to our room, close the door and pray to the Father privately. And God who sees us praying in secret will reward us. (See Matthew 6:6.)

Spend time alone with God. "Do not be in a hurry to leave the king's presence" (Ecclesiastes 8:3 NIV).

Prayer: Lord, you desire to spend time with us; may we desire to spend time with you. Amen

Day 91

"She would ... return to another part of the harem to the care of Shaashgaz, the king's eunuch who was in charge of the concubines" (Esther 2:14 NIV).

"When he, the Spirit of truth, is come, he will guide you into all truth" (John 16:13 KJV).

Again, we have the Holy Spirit, represented by the king's eunuch, taking care of and being in charge of Esther, who represents the church, Christ's bride.

Jesus referred to the Holy Spirit as the Spirit of truth. He said the Spirit of truth would guide us to the truth. Truth is a solid foundation that doesn't change. Truth is reality. Truth is what is, not what we perceive it to be; our perception can be wrong.

In the Bible we are told to think on things that are true. (Philippians 4:8) We are to speak the truth (Ephesians 4:15), obey the truth (1 Peter 1:22), walk in truth (3 John 1:3-4), worship in truth (John 4:23-24), and work with others for the truth (3 John 1:8).

When Jesus was being questioned by Pilate, Pilate wanted to know what truth was. The answer is: Jesus is truth. God's word is truth. (John 14:6, 17:17, 18:38)

Prayer: God, you are a God of truth; help us to walk in truth. Amen

Day 92

"She would not return to the king unless he was pleased with her and *summoned her by name*" (Esther 2:14 NIV).

"He calls his own sheep by name" (John 10:3 NIV).

God calls us by our name; he knows who we are.

One night the Lord called to the boy Samuel, who was lying down near the ark of God in the temple. Samuel answered and ran to Eli the priest who had also gone to bed. Samuel thought Eli had called him. Eli told him that he hadn't called and to go back and lie down. After this happened three times, Eli realized that Samuel was being called by the Lord. He told him to go back to bed and if he heard the voice again to tell the Lord he was listening. So Samuel went back to bed. The Lord stood by Samuel and called his name again. This time Samuel told the Lord to speak and he would listen. (See 1 Samuel 3.)

When the Lord calls our name, do we hear? Are we listening for the Lord?

Prayer: When you call, Lord, may we be listening. Amen

Day 93

"When the turn came for Esther ... to go to the king" (Esther 2:15 NIV).

"You are my King and my God" (Psalm 44:4 NIV).

The time will come when it will be our turn to go to the King.

We have been under the care of the Holy Spirit and let him be in charge of our lives. The world, the flesh and the devil tried to distract us, but we held fast to Christ. We obeyed the truth and walked in truth because we were guided by the Spirit of truth.

Our beauty treatments (the beauty of holiness) have been given to us and we have eaten our special food (the word of God and doing his will). Because we gave ourselves to God whole-heartedly and obeyed his Word, he kept us from being conformed to the world's standards. Instead, our minds were renewed and we were transformed into the image of Christ.

We submitted to the dealings of the seven attendants that he assigned (trouble, sorrow, temptation, suffering, the poor, persecution and death). We didn't want these attendants but God used them to teach us humility, kindness and perseverance. With these attendants at our side we learned to be totally dependent on the Holy Spirit.

The King is pleased with us and we have won his favor. Soon he will call our name and we will go to be with him forever.

Prayer: We are waiting for you, our God and King. Amen

Esther Chapter 2

Day 94

"(The young woman Mordecai had adopted, the daughter of his uncle Abihail)" (Esther 2:15 NIV).

We have "received the Spirit of adoption, whereby we cry, Abba, Father" (Romans 8:15 KJV).

We were without God and had no hope, when God, through his son Jesus, rescued us and adopted us into his family. (See Ephesians 1:5, 2:12) God could have left us to our own devices, wandering around lost and without purpose or direction. But he had mercy on us and chose us to be adopted into his family forever.

We have a worldwide family of brothers and sisters in Christ. Throughout the generations and in countries around the globe, God has been at work drawing people to himself and who have become part of his family. God is the ultimate "family man"; he does the term "father" proud.

Prayer: God, thank you that you adopted us into your family and you are our Father. Amen

Day 95

"She asked for nothing other than what Hegai, the king's eunuch who was in charge of the harem, suggested" (Esther 2:15 NIV).

"The Spirit itself [makes] intercession for us" (Romans 8:26 KJV).

When we pray, we can ask for what the Holy Spirit suggests. In our humanness we don't always know what to ask for, or how to pray about a situation, but the Holy Spirit can direct us in our prayers. The Spirit can also pray for us when we can't find the words to pray. (See Romans 8:26-27.)

Sometimes we may have doubts about whether God is really with us. "The Spirit itself [bears] witness with our spirit, that we are the children of God" (Romans 8:16 KJV). His Spirit in us confirms we are his. And, as it says later in that chapter that nothing can separate us from God's love.

If we feel he is far away, we can ask the Spirit to search our hearts to see if there is a sin that needs to be repented of and forgiven. (See Psalm 139:23-24.) If nothing comes to our minds, we can go on in faith, not depending on our feelings. (See Hebrews 11:1.)

Prayer: Holy Spirit, when we are in doubt, assure us of your presence within. Amen

"And Esther won the favor of everyone who saw her" (Esther 2:15 NIV).

The disciples were "praising God and enjoying the favor of all the people" (Acts 2:47 NIV).

For a time, the early church found favor with the people. All were astonished at the miracles being performed by the apostles. The believers were gathering for prayer and fellowship and daily people were being saved.

It's easy to praise God when things are going well and people are supportive and favorable to us. But what about when people turn against us or our circumstances are painful?

Paul and Silas delivered a woman from bondage. This made her owners mad and then the crowd joined in with harassing them. They had Paul and Silas arrested; their clothes were stripped off and they were beaten with rods. Then their feet were put in stocks and they were under guard. What did they do? "At midnight Paul and Silas prayed, and sang praises unto God: and the prisoners heard them" (Acts 16:25 KJV). Not only were they rejoicing in their sufferings but also being a witness to those around them, showing them that God is "a very present help in trouble" (Psalm 46:1 KJV). (See Acts 16:16-40 for the whole story.)

Prayer: Lord, help us to rejoice in you in all circumstances. Amen

Day 97

"She was taken to King Xerxes in the royal residence in the tenth month, the month of Tebeth, in *the seventh* year of his reign" (Esther 2:16 NIV).

"One shall be taken" (Matthew 24:40 KJV).

Esther was taken to the king. We also shall be taken, in death or taken up to meet the Lord in the air. Now is the time to be preparing for that day. We need to live wisely and take advantage of the time we have to serve God in this wicked world. (See Ephesians 5:15-16.)

Here are examples from the Scriptures of those taken up to heaven alive:

Enoch walked closely with God and then one day, God took him. (Genesis 5:24)

Elijah was taken to heaven by a chariot and horses of fire. (2 Kings 2:11)

Jesus went up in a cloud. (Acts 1:9)

Believers at the return of Christ will rise to meet him. (1 Thessalonians 4:16-17)

Two prophets in the future, will be killed, brought back to life and go up to heaven. (Revelation 11:7-12)

Notice the number seven again, (in Esther 2:16) meaning completion. God takes us (in death) when we have completed our time on earth according to his timetable, not ours. (See Psalm 31:15.)

Prayer: Lord, prepare our hearts to meet you. Amen

"And the king loved Esther above all the women, and she obtained grace and [favor] in his sight more than all the virgins" (Esther 2:17 KJV).

"Mary; you have found favor with God" (Luke 1:30 NIV).

Just as Esther, the virgin, found favor with the king; Mary, the virgin, found favor with God.

Mary was a young woman engaged to be married to Joseph. An angel visited her and told her that the Lord was with her and he had found favor with her. The angel told her not to be afraid and that God had chosen her to carry his Son. She was to name him Jesus. Mary agreed to God's plan; she rejoiced in the Lord.

We may not be visited by an angel like Mary, but the Lord can and does speak to us from his Word and the Holy Spirit. We have found favor with God by believing in his Son. We continue to have favor with God by obeying him just as Mary obeyed him. We have a closer relationship with him as we listen to his voice and follow his commands.

Prayer: Lord, may we agree to your plans for our lives as Mary agreed to your plan. Amen

Day 99

"He set the royal crown upon her head, and made her queen instead of Vashti" (Esther 2:17 KJV).

"I put ... a beautiful crown on your head" (Ezekiel 16:12 NIV).

Just as the king set a crown on Esther's head, the Bible says that God's followers also will have crowns. Those who remain faithful to God will receive a crown of righteousness and a crown of life. (See 2 Timothy 4:8; James 1:12.) In Revelation 3:11, Jesus tells the church to hold on to their faith, so they won't lose their crowns and to be ready for his soon coming.

The royal crown represents the position and authority given her by the king. Esther (Christ's bride) receives the royal crown that Vashti (the wicked) lost. The royal position and authority that Vashti lost represents what was lost when Adam and Eve sinned in the Garden. Satan usurped authority over the human race, because of sin; but Christ won it back for us, if we will receive it.

Prayer: Thank you, Lord, that if we are faithful to you till death, we will receive a crown of life. Amen

Day 100

"And the king gave a great banquet, Esther's banquet, for all his nobles and officials" (Esther 2:18 NIV).

"Let us be glad and rejoice, and give [honor] to him: for the marriage of the Lamb is come, and his wife [has] made herself ready. ... Blessed are they which are called unto the marriage supper of the Lamb" (Revelation 19:7, 9 KJV).

Esther's banquet, given by the king, represents the marriage supper of the Lamb. (See also the parable in Matthew 22:1-14.)

"And to her [the bride] was granted that she should be arrayed in fine linen, clean and white: for the fine linen is the righteousness of saints" (Revelation 19:8 KJV).

The bride is ready; Christ, the Lamb is come—let the feast begin.

A note of explanation: King Xerxes represents God: Father, Son and Holy Spirit. In this study of the Book of Esther, we see the Son and Holy Spirit step down, so to speak, and play added roles. (Actually, this really did happen: Christ stepped down and lived among us, and the Holy Spirit came down to live within us.) Mordecai in this story represents Christ but has a fatherly role with Esther. Esther (Church) is the bride of the king (God, the Son.)

Prayer: Lord, make us ready for this great event of the banquet in heaven. Amen

Day 101

"He proclaimed a holiday throughout the provinces and distributed gifts with royal liberality" (Esther 2:18 NIV).

He "gave gifts unto men" (Ephesians 4:8 KJV).

God has generously given gifts to all of us. Some of the spiritual gifts listed in Romans 12 are: prophesying, serving others, teaching the word of God, encouraging the believers and giving to those in need. (See 1 Corinthians 12:1-11 for more gifts of the Spirit.)

In Ephesians 4, it says that when Christ went to heaven, he also gave us these gifts for the building up of the Church:

Apostles: Those who are sent out to do the miraculous works of God. (2 Corinthians 12:12)

Prophets: They speak words (prophecies) given by God for his people. (Romans 12:6)

Evangelists: Those who are called to travel about sharing the gospel of Jesus to the lost. (2 Timothy 4:2, 5)

Pastors: They act as a shepherd or caregiver to a certain group of believers. (Acts 20:28)

Teachers: Those who teach the Bible to others. (Acts 18:11)

These leaders are for the "perfecting of the saints, for the work of the ministry, [and] for the edifying of the body of Christ" (Ephesians 4:12 KJV).

Prayer: Thank you, God, for the gifts you liberally give to your church. Amen

"And when the virgins were gathered together the second time" (Esther 2:19 KJV).

"At that time the kingdom of heaven will be like ten virgins who took their lamps and went out to meet the bridegroom" (Matthew 25:1 NIV).

The first time the virgins were assembled (Esther 2:8) they were put under the care of Hegai (Holy Spirit) for twelve months of beauty treatments (purification and refining). Now they are assembled the second time.

Jesus told this parable about virgins who were gathered together:

There were ten virgins, five were wise and five were foolish. They were all waiting for the bridegroom. The foolish didn't take extra oil for their lamps and their lamps were going out because the bridegroom didn't come right away. The wise had brought extra oil; so when the bridegroom finally came, they were well prepared. The wise went with him to the wedding banquet, but the foolish were shut out. (See Matthew 25:1-13.)

The moral of the story is to be ready for the Lord's return; it may seem afar off, but be ready, for you do not know when he will return.

Prayer: Lord, help us not to be like the foolish virgins who weren't prepared for the long wait but to be wise and persevere until you come.

Day 103

"Then Mordecai sat in the king's gate" (Esther 2:19 KJV).

Jesus said, "I am the gate for the sheep" and "I am the gate; whoever enters through me will be saved" (John 10:7, 9 NIV).

Mordecai, who represents Christ, sits at the king's gate because you have to pass through him to get to the king. Jesus said, "I am the way and the truth and the life. No one comes to the Father except through me" (John 14:6 NIV). Jesus is the only means by which we can reach the Father. Many will try to find God through different religions or through their good works; neither will make it. Only through believing in the Son of God who sacrificed himself for our sins will we be accepted by the Father.

Prayer: Jesus, we believe you are the only way to the Father, we put our trust in you. Amen

Day 104

"But Esther had kept secret her family background and nationality just as Mordecai had told her to do" (Esther 2:20 NIV).

"To [everything] there is a season. ... a time to keep silence, and a time to speak" (Ecclesiastes 3:1, 7 KJV).

Esther is keeping quiet right now about her family, but later on, Mordecai will ask Esther to reveal this secret.

There are times we need to keep quiet about things the Lord is telling us so that we don't rush ahead of him. Taking the time to pray and search the word of God for direction and clarity is good. We may want to ask a trusted, godly friend to pray on our behalf about what we feel the Lord is directing us to do.

Other times someone may approach us with an opportunity. Before we give an answer, we should "first seek the counsel of the LORD" (2 Chronicles 18:4 NIV).

Prayer: Father, give us wisdom to follow you and not run ahead or lag behind. Amen

Day 105

"For she continued to follow Mordecai's instructions as she had done when he was bringing her up" (Esther 2:20 NIV).

"So then, just as you received Christ Jesus as Lord, continue to live your lives in him, rooted and built up in him, strengthened in the faith as you were taught" (Colossians 2:6-7 NIV).

Esther respected Mordecai and followed his advice even as an adult.

No matter how mature or grown up we are in the Lord we are still to follow Christ's instructions in the Word and be led by the Spirit of God.

In Matthew 5, Jesus told his disciples:

You are the light in this world. Don't hide it. You need to shine it, by doing good so that others may see and give glory to God.

If you are at odds with a brother or sister, make things right.

When there is trouble between you and another party, try to settle things among yourselves so you don't end up in court.

Don't swear, just answer yes or no.

Love your enemies and pray for them. God loves his enemies—you once were one.

Prayer: Lord, help us to continue to follow your instructions in your Word. Amen

"During the time Mordecai was sitting at the king's gate, Bigthana and Teresh, *two of the king's officers* who guarded the doorway, became angry and *conspired to assassinate King Xerxes*" (Esther 2:21 NIV).

"The beast [Antichrist] was given a mouth to utter proud words and blasphemies. ... A second beast [false prophet]. ... performed great signs" (Revelation 13:5, 11, 13 NIV).

These two officers that planned to assassinate the king represent the Antichrist and the false prophet who will come on the world scene at the end of the age. This man, the Antichrist, will rise in power over all the nations of the world to deceive them and they will fall for his deception. "And all that dwell upon the earth shall worship him, whose names are not written in the book of life" (Revelation 13:8 KJV). He will sit in power in the temple and say he is God.

The false prophet will perform miraculous acts by the power of Satan and will deceive many. An idol will be erected in honor of the beast and those who don't worship the idol will be killed. He will force all people "to receive a mark on their right hands or on their foreheads, so that they [can't] buy or sell unless they [have] the mark, which is the name of the beast" (Revelation 13:16-17 NIV). (See 2 Thessalonians 2:3-4; Revelation 13.)

Prayer: Lord, keep us safe from deception and the lies of the enemy. Amen

Day 107

"But Mordecai found out about the plot and told Queen Esther, who in turn reported it to the king, giving credit to Mordecai" (Esther 2:22 NIV).

"The beast [Antichrist], and the kings of the earth, and their armies, gathered together to make war against [Jesus] that sat on the horse, and against his army" (Revelation 19:19 KJV).

Christ and his army from heaven will wage war against the Antichrist and his army and Christ will be victorious! (See Revelation 19:11-19.) A quick summary follows:

Heaven is opened and Jesus appears on a white horse; his eyes are like fire and he is wearing many crowns and a sword is coming from his mouth to strike down the nations. His clothing is a robe that was dipped in blood and his name is the Word of God. And with him is his army from heaven; they are dressed in white robes and are mounted on white horses. Jesus has this name written on his robe: KING OF KINGS AND LORD OF LORDS. They go to war against the beast and the kings of the nations and their armies on the earth.

Prayer: Thank you, God, for this glimpse into the future. You are the mighty God. Amen

Day 108

"And when the report was investigated and found to be true, the two officials were impaled on poles" (Esther 2:23 NIV).

"But the beast was captured, and with it the false prophet who had performed the signs on his behalf. ... The two of them were thrown alive in to the fiery lake of burning sulfur" (Revelation 19:20 NIV).

The Antichrist and false prophet were thrown into the lake of fire and their armies were killed by the sword of Christ that came from his mouth.

Later, when the season for Satan's activity is all over, the devil and all of God's enemies will be thrown in the lake of fire and "shall be tormented day and night for ever and ever" (Revelation 20:10 KJV).

When we look around and see all the wickedness and injustice in the world, it is discouraging and heartbreaking. Those who don't know what the Bible says would naturally think that evil wins—that bad people have an advantage: they get what they want. But God, who sees all, will one day correct all the wrong and all the injustice that plagues our world. Everyone, no matter how big and bad they appeared on earth, will answer to him for all they have done. (See Psalm 37.)

Prayer: Lord, thank you that you will bring this difficult season to a close. May your name be glorified. Amen

Day 109

"All this was recorded in the book of the annals in the presence of the king" (Esther 2:23, NIV).

"The dead were judged according to what they had done as recorded in the books" (Revelation 20:12 NIV). And this takes place "in the presence of God and of Christ Jesus, who will judge the living and the dead" (2 Timothy 4:1 NIV).

All people from every nation will stand before God to be judged and the books with the record of each person's life will be opened. Also, the book of life will be opened and those whose names are not in the book of life are thrown into the lake of fire. (See Revelation 20:12-15.)

"And I saw a great white throne, and him that sat on it. ... And I saw the dead, small and great, stand before God; and the books were opened: and another book was opened, which is the book of life: and the dead were judged out of those things which were written in the books, according to their works" (Revelation 20:11-12 KJV).

Prayer: Lord, forgive our sins and cleanse us so that we may stand before you on judgment day and be counted worthy to be in the Lamb's book of life. Amen

Chapter 2 Review

Day 55: Turn to God while you are young; don't put it off.

Day 65: We are to take our thoughts captive: have them under control, by the help of the Holy Spirit.

Day 67: The Lord wants us to be totally dependent on him.

Day 68: God's beauty queens look different from the world's beauty queens.

Day 83: Our nationality and family background don't matter to God; his salvation is for all.

Day 90: Spend time alone with God.

Day 97: God takes us (in death) when we have completed our time on earth according to his timetable, not ours.

Day 103: Jesus is the only means by which we can reach the Father. Many people will try to find God through different religions or through their good works; neither will make it.

Day 105: Love your enemies and pray for them. God loves his enemies—you once were one.

Prayer: Lord, we put our lives in your hands, do with us what you will. Amen

Day 111

Chapter 2 Challenge

Fill in the blank.

1. A search was made for _____ _____. (2:2)

2. The new queen would be one who _____ the king. (2:4)

3. In Susa there was a Jew from the tribe of_____, whose name was_____. (2:5)

4. He had a cousin named _____ or Esther. (2:7)

5. Esther was the king's favorite so he put a _____ on her head. (2:17)

6. The king hosted another banquet called _____ _____. (2:18)

7. _____ was often found sitting at the gate of the king's palace. (2:19)

8. While at the king's gate he overheard an _____ conspiracy. (2:21)

9. He reported it to _____ and she told ___ _____. (2:22)

Prayer: Lord, may we please you our King. Amen

"After these events, *King Xerxes honored Haman* son of Hammedatha, the Agagite, *elevating him and giving him a seat of honor higher than that of all the other nobles*" (Esther 3:1 NIV).

Satan is "the prince of this world" (John 12:31 KJV).

Haman, who represents Satan, once held a place of honor with God but was thrown out of heaven. God has allowed Satan and his cohorts (the angels who fell with him) to have power in this world. (See Revelation 12:7-10.) Satan is God's tool to test and try the hearts of all people. Satan has limited power for a limited time because God has given it to him. God is all powerful for all time.

In the future, Satan will be bound in the bottomless pit for a thousand years. During this time Christ will rule and reign on the earth. When the thousand years are up, Satan will be set free for a short time. Then he will deceive the nations and gather an army prepared to go to war against God's people. God will send down fire on the devil and his army and they will be destroyed. Then Satan will be put in the lake of fire. (See Revelation 20.)

Prayer: Thank you, God, that you are more powerful than the enemy. You will deal with Satan and he will not harm your people any more. Amen

Day 113

"All the royal officials at the king's gate knelt down *and paid honor to Haman*, for the king had commanded this concerning him" (Esther 3:2 NIV).

"If the LORD be God, follow him: but if Baal, then follow him" (1 Kings 18:21 KJV).

People pay honor to Satan when they follow him knowingly or unknowingly. As to whom to follow, there are only two choices – God or Satan. Satan often disguises himself, for the purpose of deception. (See 2 Corinthians 11:14.) He also uses the names of other "gods" people worship.

Elijah the prophet challenged the people to follow God if they really believed he was God; if not then they should go ahead and follow Baal, a false god. There was a showdown on Mount Carmel between the prophets of Baal and God's prophet Elijah. The true "God" would be determined by which one caused fire to come down from heaven. The false prophets called out to Baal all day long, but they got no response. When fire fell from heaven at Elijah's request and consumed the sacrifice on the altar, the people shouted that the Lord was God. (See 1 Kings 18:19-40.)

This verse says it all: "I am God, and there is no other" (Isaiah 46:9 NIV).

Prayer: God, you are the one and only true God. We will worship you. Amen

"But Mordecai would not kneel down or pay him honor" (Esther 3:2 NIV).

"Worship no other god: for the LORD, whose name is Jealous, is a jealous God" (Exodus 34:14 KJV).

After Jesus was baptized, he was sent into the desert by the Holy Spirit and was tempted by the devil for forty days. In one of the temptations, the devil promised Jesus that all the kingdoms of the world would be his if only he would worship him. Jesus quoted to him from the Old Testament where it says that we are to worship only God.

We are not to make movie stars, sports heroes, singers, political leaders or anyone else our idol or god. They are not worthy of our worship or wholehearted devotion—only God the Father, Son and Holy Spirit.

Mordecai (Christ) would not bow down to Haman (Satan). Jesus, our example, always chose the will of the Father; he was always loyal to Him.

Prayer: Thank you, Jesus, for not falling for the lies of the enemy and remaining true to your Father. Help us do the same. Amen

Day 115

"Then the royal officials at the king's gate asked Mordecai, 'Why do you disobey the king's command?'" (Esther 3:3 NIV).

"The Pharisees said to [Jesus], 'Look, why are they doing what is unlawful on the Sabbath?'" (Mark 2:24 NIV).

The Pharisees (the religious officials) asked Jesus why his disciples were disobeying God's command concerning the Sabbath. Jesus' disciples were picking grain to eat as they walked along a field. The religious leaders were calling it "work" and it was against God's law to work on the Sabbath. (See Mark 2:23-28.)

On another Sabbath, Jesus was at the synagogue teaching and there was a man there with a shriveled hand. The Pharisees were there and watching to see if Jesus would heal him on the Sabbath which would be "working." Jesus asked them if it was lawful to do good on the Sabbath. He then healed the man and it made the religious leaders furious. (See Luke 6:6-11.)

Prayer: Jesus, may our "work" be doing good. Amen

"Day after day they spoke to him but he refused to comply" (Esther 3:4 NIV).

Jesus "was in all points tempted like ... we are, yet without sin" (Hebrews 4:15 KJV).

Jesus understands how it feels to be tempted. He faced temptation day after day just like we do, but he refused to give in; he remained true to his Father. He didn't allow people's opinions to determine what he would do—he didn't let the crowd influence him toward evil.

Jesus' main goal in life was to please his Father in heaven. He spent much time in prayer so he could receive direction and power from God to do what he needed to do. He showed his disciples, by example, what it was like to walk each day in the will of the Father. He loved all the people he came in contact with; but that didn't mean he was a softy. He gave a strong word to those who needed to be corrected; but a kind word was given to the hurting and seeking person.

Jesus didn't rush around trying to reach everyone and fixing every wrong thing he saw. He attended to the needs God put in his path and the needs the Holy Spirit directed him to.

Prayer: Father, help us to follow the example of your Son and do your will. Amen

Day 117

"Therefore they told Haman about it to see whether Mordecai's behavior would be tolerated" (Esther 3:4 NIV).

"Then the Pharisees went out, and held a council against [Jesus], how they might destroy him" (Matthew 12:14 KJV).

After Jesus had healed the man with the shriveled hand on the Sabbath, the Pharisees had a meeting to plan how to kill him. The Pharisees were highly respected and they didn't like Jesus coming in and challenging their authority. They knew the law of God backwards and forwards and Jesus didn't always do what they thought he should.

In Matthew 23, Jesus publicly exposed the Pharisees and the religious leaders for their pretense—for not doing what they told others to do. He even called them names like blind guides, hypocrites and fools. Of course, the Pharisees didn't like it. According to them, this behavior of Jesus was not to be tolerated.

Prayer: Lord, help us to do good even when it's not appreciated by others. We want your approval, not the approval of people.

Day 118

"For he had told them he was a Jew" (Esther 3:4 NIV).
"You are a Jew" (John 4:9 NIV).

Jesus encountered a Samaritan woman at a well and asked her to give him a drink of water. She was surprised that he talked to her. (Jews didn't have anything to do with the Samaritans.) He challenged her by offering her living water. After talking with him she believed he was the promised Messiah.

She left him and went back to her town and told her friends and neighbors about this man Jesus. Many of them believed, also. The townspeople went looking for Jesus and asked him to stay; so he stayed for two days, telling them about the kingdom of God. They said, "We have heard him ourselves, and know that this is indeed the Christ, the [Savior] of the world" (John 4:42 KJV). (See also John 4:7-30, 39-42.)

Prayer: Jesus, may we tell others that you are the Savior of the world. Amen

Day 119

"When Haman saw that Mordecai would not kneel down or pay him honor, he was enraged" (Esther 3:5 NIV).

"Then Nebuchadnezzar in his rage and fury commanded [them] to bring Shadrach, Meshach, and Abednego" (Daniel 3:13 KJV).

In Daniel 3, King Nebuchadnezzar was furious when the three Hebrews: Shadrach, Meshach and Abednego, would not bow down and worship the image of gold he had erected. They refused because one of the Ten Commandments (see Exodus 20:4-5) says not to make idols and bow down to them. They were only to bow down to the true God.

Their punishment was to be thrown in a fiery furnace. They were bound and thrown in. Later, the three men were brought out and they were not burned; they didn't even smell like smoke. The king then made a law that no one was to speak against the God of the Hebrews.

Prayer: Thank you, God, for showing this king your mighty power by protecting your servants. Amen

"Yet having learned who Mordecai's people were" (Esther 3:6 NIV).

"By this everyone will know that you are my disciples, if you love one another" (John 13:35 NIV).

Everyone will learn who Jesus' people are by how his disciples love others.

In 1 Corinthians 13, Paul says we can have spiritual gifts like prophecy, words of knowledge or great faith, but if we don't have love, we've gained nothing. We can give to the poor and sacrifice our lives, but without love, it does us no good.

Love is patient and kind. It's not envious of others or proud. It doesn't put others down or act selfishly. Love doesn't get angry quickly and it doesn't keep count of how many times a person wrongs us. Love is happy about the things that are true and right. It is trustworthy, hopeful and enduring in all situations.

To love is to succeed. Love is the definition of success because God is love.

Prayer: Lord, help us to love because when we love we are being like you. Amen

Day 121

"[Haman] scorned the idea of killing only Mordecai" (Esther 3:6 NIV).

Saul was threatening to kill off the Lord's disciples. (See Acts 9:1.)

Saul was a man on a mission; he thought he was doing this for God: he was hunting down disciples of Jesus. He had received papers from the high priest that gave him authority to find these people of the Way and arrest them and take them to Jerusalem. On the way to Damascus, he was blinded by a bright light and he fell to the ground. Jesus spoke to him and Saul was changed forever. Even his name changed to Paul.

Right away Paul started preaching about Jesus. He spent the rest of his life traveling near and far sharing the gospel, planting new churches and writing to the churches from prison. Thirteen of our New Testament books of the Bible are attributed to Paul.

Wickedness as well as good starts with an idea. Haman's idea to kill Mordecai and the Jews was certainly from the devil. The Bible wisely says, "Keep [your] heart with all diligence; for out of it are the issues of life" (Proverbs 4:23 KJV).

Prayer: Lord, you are able to save even the most unlikely person and use them for your glory. We give you praise. Amen

"Instead Haman looked for a way to destroy all Mordecai's people, the Jews, throughout the whole kingdom of Xerxes" (Esther 3:6 NIV).

"Saul began to destroy the church" (Acts 8:3 NIV).

Saul was trying to destroy the church. Satan wants to destroy all of God's people. In the Book of Acts, we see great persecution against the Christians: Stephan is stoned, James is slain with a sword, Saul arrests men and women and puts them in prison because they are Christ's followers. In Hebrews 11, it tells the history of some of the righteous: they were tortured, beaten, chained and put in prison, stoned, sawed in two, and forced to hide in caves.

Jesus said those whose holy living causes them to be persecuted are blessed and will inherit the kingdom of heaven. When they are insulted and slandered because of following Christ, they are to rejoice because they will be greatly rewarded in heaven. The prophets of old were persecuted also. (See Matthew 5:10-12.)

Persecution has not stopped. Christians are persecuted around the world.

Prayer: Lord, remind your people to pray for the persecuted church. Amen

Day 123

"In the twelfth year of King Xerxes, in the first month, the month of Nisan, *the pur (that is, the lot) was cast in the presence of Haman* to select a day and month. And the lot fell on the twelfth month, the month of Adar" (Esther 3:7 NIV).

"And they crucified him, and [divided] his garments, casting lots [dice]" (Matthew 27:35 KJV).

In Haman's plot against Mordecai a lot was cast, and at Christ's crucifixion lots were cast. Hundreds of years before, King David prophesied about this happening to the Messiah. "They part my garments among them, and cast lots upon my vesture" (Psalm 22:18 KJV).

In Acts 1, the disciples are gathered together and Peter quotes from Psalm 109:8 where it states that another disciple is to take Judas' place. (He betrayed Jesus and killed himself.) So, the disciples chose two faithful followers of Jesus, Justus and Matthias. "And they [cast] their lots; and the lot fell upon Matthias; and he was numbered with the eleven apostles" (Acts 1:26 KJV).

Prayer: Thank you, Jesus, for dying for us, so that we might live. Amen

Day 124

"Then Haman said to King Xerxes, *'There is a certain people dispersed among the peoples in all the provinces of your kingdom'*" (Esther 3:8 NIV).

"They were all scattered abroad throughout the regions" (Acts 8:1 KJV).

Stephen, a man full of the Holy Spirit, was martyred for his faith. "And at that time there was a great persecution against the church which was at Jerusalem; and they were all scattered abroad throughout the regions of Judaea and Samaria, except the apostles. ... [And] they that were scattered abroad went [everywhere] preaching the word" (Acts 8:1, 4 KJV).

God used what seemed like a bad thing, persecution, to spread the message of the gospel to the different regions. Because of their witness and the witness of those after them, there are believers even today dispersed among people all over the world.

Prayer: Thank you, God, for the witness and boldness of the early church to spread the gospel. Thank you for believers down through the ages who have done the same. Amen

Day 125

"Who keep themselves separate" (Esther 3:8 NIV).

"Come out from among them, and be ... separate," says the Lord. (2 Corinthians 6:17 KJV).

Paul the Apostle exhorted the believers not to socialize with immoral and sinful people; he wasn't referring to the unsaved people; he meant don't keep company with someone who calls himself a Christian and is immoral and living a life of sin—don't even eat with them. (See 1 Corinthians 5:9-11.)

There are times we have to separate ourselves from activities or gatherings that would not be pleasing to the Lord—our presence there may be taken as a sign of support for that activity. We need to ask the Holy Spirit to give us discernment for when to participate and when to abstain. Also, the Lord may permit one person to do something and another not to do the very same thing. He knows our strengths and weaknesses, so he will guide accordingly.

Prayer: Lord, help us to follow the leading of your Spirit so that we may be a holy people. Amen

"Their customs are different from those of all other people" (Esther 3:8 NIV).

"You must not live according to the customs of the nations" (Leviticus 20:23 NIV).

The Jews were different than those around them; Christians should be different than the worldly people around them. Our difference shouldn't be just that we go to church. Our faith should be a daily experience of following the teachings of Jesus. Jesus said, "Let your light so shine before men, that they may see your good works, and glorify your Father which is in heaven" (Matthew 5:16 KJV).

Hopefully as believers we will be different in the sense that honesty and integrity will be of utmost importance to us. May our complaints be few and our thankfulness abundant. May we be alert to the needs of others and be a help to them.

True followers of Christ stand out because our customs are different; we live by the standard of the Bible, not the culture.

Prayer: Lord, help us to let our light shine before others so that you will be glorified. Amen

Day 127

"And they do not obey the king's laws; it is not in the king's best interest to tolerate them" (Esther 3:8 NIV).

"We ought to obey God rather than men" (Acts 5:29 KJV).

Peter and the other apostles were told by the Jewish authorities not to preach in the name of Jesus any more. The apostles answered them by saying, "We ought to obey God rather than men." The religious leaders and the high priest were to judge matters of God's law as it concerned the Jewish people; but because they didn't accept Jesus as the Messiah this put them at odds with Christ's followers.

"When they had called the apostles, and beaten them, they commanded that they should not speak in the name of Jesus, and let them go. And they departed from the presence of the council, rejoicing that they were counted worthy to suffer shame for his name" (Acts 5:40-41 KJV). The early disciples were willing to risk imprisonment and death in order to spread the gospel of Christ.

Prayer: Lord, may this be our goal also, to obey you before others. Amen

Day 128

"If it pleases the king, let a decree be issued to destroy them" (Esther 3:9 NIV).

"The time is coming when anyone who kills you will think they are offering a service to God" (John 16:2 NIV).

Jesus warned his disciples that in the future when people killed them, they would claim that they were on a mission from God; but in fact, they don't know God or his Son. He told them this ahead of time so they wouldn't be surprised by it later and stumble and fall. Jesus knew he was not going to be with them much longer on the earth, so he was trying to prepare them for what they would face after he left. He told them he was leaving, but that he would send the Holy Spirit to be with them and in them.

Throughout history and even today Christians have been killed in the name of "God." These persecutors have been deceived; they "changed the truth of God into a lie" (Romans 1:25 KJV).

Prayer: Lord, open the eyes of the persecutors of your church to the truth so they will be saved. Amen

Day 129

"And I will give ten thousand talents of silver to the king's administrators for the royal treasury" (Esther 3:9 NIV).

"They counted out for him thirty pieces of silver" (Matthew 26:15 NIV).

Judas Iscariot, one of the twelve disciples of Jesus, was a thief. As keeper of the disciple's money he used to help himself to the funds when others weren't looking. (See John12:6.) Knowing that the chief priests and religious officials were plotting to get rid of Jesus, he went to the priests and offered to hand Jesus over to them. He asked what they were willing to pay him and they gave him thirty pieces of silver. After that, Judas kept watch to see how he could betray Jesus. (See Matthew 26:14-16.)

A price was put on the Jews' head (by Haman) and on Jesus' head. Money is a great motivator; but it can be used for evil as well as good. God needs to be our master and money our servant, not the other way around. (See Matthew 6:24.)

Prayer: Lord, deliver us from greed and covetousness. Help us to be satisfied with what you provide for us. Amen

Day 130

"And the king took his ring from his hand, and gave it unto Haman the son of Hammedatha the Agagite, *the Jews' enemy"* (Esther 3:10 KJV).

"The LORD said … they have rejected me, [so] that I should not reign over them" (1 Samuel 8:7 KJV).

The king is giving his signet ring (authority) to Haman to destroy the Jews. This represents God giving authority to Satan in this world because of people's sin.

In 1 Samuel 8, the prophet Samuel was old. So he had his sons be judges over Israel in his stead, but they were corrupt. Knowing this, the people approached Samuel and asked for a king like the other nations had. Samuel was against this; the Lord was to be their king. The Lord told Samuel to go ahead and give them a king because they had already rejected him as their king.

Whenever we reject the authority of God the enemy can gain access. Years ago the Bible was read and prayers were offered to God publicly in the school system. Then God was kicked out. Now shooters come in and kill and terrorize our children. There is a price to be paid for rejecting God and his rule over us. We have been paying that price ever since Adam and Eve's sin. The more we push God away the more the enemy comes in.

Prayer: Lord, we pray "when the enemy shall come in like a flood, [that] the Spirit of the LORD shall lift up a standard against him" (Isaiah 59:19 KJV). Amen

Day 131

"'Keep the money,' the king said to Haman" (Esther 3:11 NIV).

"May your money perish with you" (Acts 8:20 NIV).

God's will or power cannot be bought.

In the city of Samaria there was a man named Simon. Simon practiced sorcery and amazed the people so much that they thought he had the power of God. When Philip came and preached the gospel of the kingdom in Samaria many believed and were baptized, even Simon the sorcerer. Simon followed Philip everywhere and was astonished at the miracles performed by Philip through the power of God.

The Apostles Peter and John arrived and prayed for the new believers to receive the Holy Spirit. When Simon saw this, he offered Peter and John money so that he could obtain the power to impart the Spirit as they had done. Peter rebuked Simon and told him to repent and hope the Lord would forgive him. Simon then asked Peter to pray for him. (See Acts 8:9-24.)

Prayer: Lord, keep our hearts pure and free from the pursuit of power. Amen

Esther Chapter 3

Day 132

"And do with the people as you please" (Esther 3:11 NIV).

"The LORD said unto Satan, Behold, he is in [your] hand; but save his life'" (Job 2:6 KJV).

Job was a righteous man, one who followed God and lived a blameless life. Yet God gave Satan permission to strike Job's body; which he did, but Job still remained faithful to God. Even during his great suffering Job cried, "Though [God] slay me, yet will I trust in him" (Job 13:15 KJV).

We can live lives wholly dedicated to God, but that doesn't mean that tragedy, failure or sickness won't visit us. We can read about Job and be warned that hard times will come. Hopefully, our response will be like Job's, to trust God even if we don't see what we did wrong or why we should have to go through this trial. God brought Job through and blessed him with twice as much as he had before. God may not give us double of what we lost, but he will bless us for trusting in him.

Haman (Satan) was given permission from the king (God) to do as he pleased with the Jews (Job).

Prayer: Lord, may our faith not falter in hard times, hold us steady. Amen

Day 133

"Then on the thirteenth day of the first month the *royal secretaries were summoned*" (Esther 3:12 NIV).

"Bless the LORD, [you] his angels, that excel in strength, that do his commandments, hearkening unto the voice of his word" (Psalm 103:20 KJV).

The royal secretaries represent God's angels.

Throughout the Bible from Genesis to Revelation we see God's "royal secretaries" at work. The Bible tells us of two incidents in Jesus' life where angels ministered to him: once after his time of testing in the desert and again when he prayed in the garden before he was arrested. (See Matthew 4:11; Luke 22:43.)

When Jesus was arrested, Peter tried to save him by drawing his sword. Jesus told Peter to put his sword away; he could ask his Father to send a huge number of angels to help him if he wanted. (See Matthew 26:51-53.) Jesus didn't call for the angels to save him; he went to the cross to save us. He chose to save us instead of himself.

Prayer: Thank you, Lord, for the ministry of the angels from heaven. Amen

"They wrote out in the script of each province and in the language of each people all Haman's orders to the king's satraps, the governors of the various provinces, and the nobles of the various peoples. *These were written in the name of King Xerxes himself and sealed with his own ring*" (Esther 3:12 NIV).

"When you believed, you were marked in him with a seal, the promised Holy Spirit, who is a deposit guaranteeing our inheritance" (Ephesians 1:13-14 NIV).

After hearing the gospel and believing in Christ as the sacrifice for our sins, we are sealed by the Holy Spirit. Jesus said, "I give unto them eternal life; and they shall never perish, neither shall any man pluck them out of my hand" (John 10:28 KJV). We are secure in him unless we turn away. He never deserts us; we are the ones who desert him. (See Hebrews 3:12, 14, 13:5.)

In the Book of Revelation, the Apostle John saw in a vision, angels sent to seal the followers of God. "And I saw another angel ascending from the east, having the seal of the living God: and he cried with a loud voice ... "Saying, Hurt not the earth, neither the sea, nor the trees, till we have sealed the servants of our God in their foreheads" (Revelation 7:2-3 KJV).

Prayer: Thank you, God, that we are sealed by you and safe in your care. Amen

Day 135

"Dispatches were sent by couriers to all the king's provinces with the order to destroy, kill and annihilate all the Jews— young and old, women and children—on a single day, the thirteenth day of the twelfth month, the month of Adar, and to plunder their goods" (Esther 3:13 NIV).

"The thief [comes] ... to steal, and to kill, and to destroy" (John 10:10 KJV).

The Jews' enemy Haman represents Satan, who only wants to steal, kill and destroy. Satan wants to steal and destroy our faith in God, and sometimes he is successful. "For some are already turned aside after Satan" (1 Timothy 5:15 KJV).

Jesus told Peter that Satan was going to try to trip Peter up, but he was praying that he would not lose his faith. (See Luke 22:31-32.) Jesus knew Peter was going to fail this test, just as he knows we will sometimes fail. We need to repent like Peter—get up and continue to follow Christ. In him is forgiveness and restoration.

Prayer: Lord, when we fail please forgive us and restore us to yourself. Amen

"To destroy … [the] young" (Esther 3:13 NIV).

"The young men and young women will perish" (Deuteronomy 32:25 NIV).

Satan is trying to destroy our young people, and too often succeeding. He is attacking their bodies, minds and souls through drugs, alcohol, eating disorders, violence, suicide and more. They are being influenced by a society run amok. "Woe unto them that call evil good, and good evil; that put darkness for light, and light for darkness" (Isaiah 5:20 KJV). Our young people need the Truth before they are hooked on the lies they are constantly exposed to.

"Even the youths shall faint and be weary, and the young men shall utterly fall: But they that wait upon the LORD shall renew their strength; they shall mount up with wings as eagles; they shall run, and not be weary; and they shall walk, and not faint" (Isaiah 40:30-31 KJV).

Prayer: Father, let your Word ring true in the hearts of our youth so they will come to you. Amen

Day 137

"To destroy ... [the] old ... and to plunder their goods" (Esther 3:13 NIV).

"Cast me not off in the time of old age; forsake me not when my strength [fails]" (Psalm 71:9 KJV).

The old are being destroyed by neglect; many are forsaken by family and put in nursing homes and left. The older folks still in their own homes are falling prey to scams by con men who wish to plunder their goods. Blessed are those who have family or friends that will go to the grocery store for them, carry them to the doctor and sit with them to help ease their loneliness.

The elderly who are terminally ill are quietly being eliminated by "mercy killings." This may be more common than we think. Do those who abuse the elderly not think that one day they may be old, sick and as helpless as the ones they prey on?

May the Lord not forsake us when we are old and gray. (See Psalm 71:18.)

Prayer: Lord, may you be with those who are old and alone. Comfort them, Father. May those who are able come along beside them to help. Amen

Day 138

"To destroy ... [the] women" (Esther 3:13 NIV).

"Why are you bothering this woman?" (Matthew 26:10 NIV).

Jesus asked his disciples why they were causing trouble for this woman when she was honoring him by anointing him with expensive oil. In that day and culture women were not highly respected, but Jesus often showed them compassion. One day when Jesus saw a widow, whose only son had just died, he had compassion on her and raised her son from the dead. He delivered Mary Magdalene from evil spirits, and he offered living water to a Samaritan woman. (See Luke 7:12, 8:2; John 4:10.)

Women are also at risk today. There are women being beaten, abused and killed in their homes. Some are assaulted at their workplaces, others accosted on the streets and raped. They all need God's help and healing. "He [heals] the broken in heart, and [binds] up their wounds" (Psalm 147:3 KJV).

Prayer: Father, bring help, healing, hope and salvation to women around the world. Amen

Day 139

"To destroy ... [the] children" (Esther 3:13 NIV).

"And they brought young children to him ... and his disciples rebuked those that brought them" (Mark 10:13 KJV).

People brought their children to Jesus so that he might bless them, but the disciples tried to stop this. When Jesus saw what his disciples were doing, he told them to let the children come because they are part of the kingdom of God. Jesus said that only those with childlike faith would enter his kingdom.

Jairus, a religious ruler, came to Jesus and asked him to come and heal his twelve-year-old daughter who was dying. As Jesus followed the man to his house, someone came to Jairus to report that his daughter had already died. So Jesus didn't need to come. Jesus told Jairus not to fear but to believe, and they continued on to his house. When they got there, Jesus took the girl's hand and raised her to life again. (See Mark 5:22-24, 35-43.) This is how God feels about little children.

How are children treated today? There are those who are loved and cared for; others are destroyed (by abortion) before they even take their first breath. Unfortunately, too many are neglected, beaten, abused, and murdered.

Jesus said, "Take heed that [you] despise not one of these little ones; for I say unto you, That in heaven their angels do always behold the face of my Father" (Matthew 18:10 KJV).

Prayer: Lord, send your angels to protect the little children. Amen

"A copy of the text of the edict was to be issued" (Esther 3:14 NIV).

"He sent his word" (Psalm 107:20 KJV).

The text represents the Bible. God sent his word:

Noah preached about the flood that was coming; he told the people to repent and turn to God. (2 Peter 2:5)

Moses told the people that God heard their cries and would deliver them from the Egyptians. (Exodus 3:7-8)

Gideon roused his army saying, "Wake up! God will give us victory over the Midianites!" (Judges 7:15)

The child Samuel spoke the word of the Lord to Eli the priest that judgement was coming to his family because of their wickedness. (1 Samuel 3:18)

John the Baptist spoke about the coming Messiah. (Matthew 3:3)

Jesus warned his disciples of the persecution that was to come in the last days. (Matthew 24:9)

Prayer: Thank you, Lord, that you send your word to your people. Amen

Day 141

"As law in every province and made known to the people of every nationality" (Esther 3:14 NIV).

"And the gospel must first be preached to all nations" (Mark 13:10 NIV).

Modern technology makes this more possible today than at any time in history.

Today the gospel is proclaimed in books, movies, billboards, tracts, internet sites, songs, magazines, TV, radio, T-shirts, bumper stickers and more.

We have this promise in Isaiah 55:11, that his Word that goes out will work toward the purpose that he intended. May we pray that God would soften the hearts of the people that hear it. And pray that the Holy Spirit would draw the unsaved person to the Lord. Pray that God's word would encourage the believer that is discouraged.

Prayer: "Our Father in heaven, hallowed be your name, your kingdom come, your will be done, on earth, as it is in heaven" (Matthew 6:9-10 NIV). Amen

"So they would be ready for that day" (Esther 3:14 NIV).

"Be ready, because the the Son of man will come at an hour when you do not expect him" (Matthew 24:44 NIV).

Jesus told a parable about a farmer scattering seeds. The seeds were God's word. Some seeds fell on the path and were trampled and the birds came and ate them. This is like the people who hear the Word but the devil snatches it away before they can believe.

The seeds that fell on rocky ground sprang up quickly but soon withered. This represents those who hear the Word and believe it but it doesn't take root. When trouble and hard times come, they fall away from the faith.

Some seeds fell in thorn bushes and the thorny plants choked out the seeds. These people start out good but then are overcome and distracted by the cares of life and the pursuit of riches or pleasures. Their spiritual life is slowly choked out.

Some seeds fell on good soil. These are the ones who hear God's word, believe it, obey it and their lives produce good fruit. They have a good heart, one that seeks after God. (See Luke 8:5-15.)

Are we good soil? Or has the world choked the life out of us? It's not too late to return to God and have a fresh start. Let's pray that the Lord will make us good soil.

Prayer: Lord, may many hearts turn to you, so they will be ready for the day of your return. Amen

Day 143

"The couriers went out" (Esther 3:15 NIV).

"Go out quickly into the streets and alleys of the town and bring in the poor, the crippled, the blind and the lame" (Luke 14:21 NIV).

In the parable of the banquet in Luke 14; the host sent out his servant again to look for those who would come to his banquet. Anyone in any condition was welcome to come.

"Spurred on by the king's command" (Esther 3:15 NIV).

"And the servant said, Lord, it is done as [you have] commanded, and yet there is room" (Luke 14:22 KJV).

There was still room so he sent the servant out again. This time the servant was sent out of town to the countryside to compel them to come to his banquet. The host wanted his house filled.

"And the edict was issued in the citadel of Susa" (Esther 3:15 NIV).

"Come; for all things are now ready" (Luke 14:17 KJV).

They needed to come now while the door was still open. (See Revelation 4:1.)

Prayer: Lord, as your disciples today go out and share the Word, draw souls to yourself. Thank you for being so patient. Amen

Day 144

"The king and Haman sat down to drink" (Esther 3:15 NIV).

"Now there was a day when the sons of God [angels] came to present themselves before the LORD, and Satan came also" (Job 1:6 KJV).

The king and Haman represent God and Satan.

On this day, the Lord mentions his faithful servant Job to Satan. Satan tells God that Job only follows him because he had given him so much. Job had thousands of sheep and camels. He had hundreds of oxen and donkeys; and many servants that took care of them. Job also had a wife, seven sons and three daughters.

The Lord gave permission to Satan to do what he wanted with Job's possessions. Soon after this, disaster strikes. In one day, Job loses his herds of animals, his servants and all ten of his children. Job responded by worshiping God and saying, "The LORD gave, and the LORD [has] taken away; blessed be the name of the LORD" (Job 1:21 KJV).

Prayer: Lord, when disaster strikes us or the ones we love, may we worship you. Amen

Day 145

"But the city of Susa was bewildered" (Esther 3:15 NIV).

"The LORD said to Satan, 'Have you considered my servant Job?'" (Job 1:8 NIV).

Are the angelic beings in heaven bewildered that God and Satan talk things over? (As in Job:1-2.) Are Good and Evil conferring together about people's lives?

Romans 11:33-34 (KJV) says, "O the depth of the riches both of the wisdom and knowledge of God! how unsearchable are his judgments, and his way past finding out! For who [has] known the mind of the Lord? or who [has] been his counselor?"

Trust in God and don't rely on your own understanding of a situation. (See Proverbs 3:5.)

God has his own ways of doing things and they are beyond our ability to comprehend.

Prayer: God, we don't understand your ways but may we trust in you anyway. Amen

Esther Chapter 3

Chapter 3 Review

Day 112: Satan is God's tool to test and try the hearts of all people.

Day 116: Jesus didn't rush around trying to reach everyone and fixing every wrong thing he saw.

Day 120: Love is the definition of success because God is love.

Day 122: True followers of Christ stand out because our customs are different; we live by the standard of the Bible, not the culture.

Day 130: Whenever we reject the authority of God the enemy can gain access.

Day 131: God's will or power cannot be bought.

Day 133: Christ chose to save us instead of himself.

Day 136: Our young people need the Truth before they are hooked on the lies they are constantly exposed to.

Prayer: God, help us to live true to you and not be swayed by the culture around us. Amen

Day 147

Chapter 3 Challenge

Multiple choice.

1. King Xerxes promoted (Hegai, Haman, or Harbona) above the other nobles. (3:1)

2. Mordecai refused to (pay the king, obey the king or speak to the king). (3:3-4)

3. Haman planned to (kill, exile or arrest) Mordecai and his people. (3:6)

4. This took place in the (third, tenth or twelfth) year of the king's reign. (3:7)

5. Haman offered the king (silver, gold or land) to fund his project. (3:9)

6. The king gave Haman (a crown, a ring or a house). (3:10)

7. The king and Haman sat down to (plan, write or drink). (3:15)

Prayer: Lord may we seek you and your Word before we make plans, so our plans will be pleasing to you. Amen

Day 148

"When Mordecai learned of all that had been done, he tore his clothes, put on sackcloth and ashes, and went out into the city, wailing loudly and bitterly" (Esther 4:1 NIV).

When Jesus saw the city of Jerusalem, he wept. (See Luke 19:41.)

As Jesus looked over Jerusalem he was grieved. He likened himself to a mother hen who wanted to gather her chicks under her wings to protect them, but they wouldn't come. (See Matthew 23:37.) Just as Mordecai was mourning over the imminent destruction of the Jews; Jesus was mourning over Jerusalem and all the Israelites who refused to accept God's love and care.

In the Old Testament from Abraham on through the prophets we see God's love for his people, the Israelites. Time and time again God raised up men and women to lead them in the way of righteousness. They followed faithfully for a while, then turned aside to other gods. Because of this, God would send trouble; they would repent and turn back to him, but it would be only a short time before they strayed again.

In time, God sent his Son to them and they rejected him. "He came unto his own, [the Jews] and his own received him not" (John 1:11 KJV).

Prayer: Lord, you are so patient, continue to draw people to yourself. Amen

Day 149

"But he went only as far as the king's gate, because *no one clothed in sackcloth was allowed to enter it*" (Esther 4:2 NIV).

"There shall be no more death, neither sorrow" (Revelation 21:4 KJV).

In the future, there will be a new world order, one which we cannot fathom. No sackcloth and mourning are allowed in the New Jerusalem. For God's people the time of mourning is over!

The Apostle John tells us about this in Revelation 21:

"And I saw a new heaven and a new earth: for the first heaven and the first earth were passed away; and there was no more sea. And I John saw the holy city, new Jerusalem, coming down from God out of heaven, prepared as a bride adorned for her husband. And I heard a great voice out of heaven saying, Behold, the tabernacle of God is with men, and he will dwell with them, and they shall be his people, and God himself shall be with them, and be their God. And God shall wipe away all tears from their eyes; and there shall be no more death, neither sorrow, nor crying, neither shall there be any more pain: for the former things are passed away. And he that sat upon the throne said, Behold, I make all things new" (Revelation 21:1-5 KJV).

Prayer: God, we are looking forward to that day when you make all things new. Amen

"In every province to which the edict and order of the king came, there was great mourning among the Jews, *with fasting*, weeping and wailing" (Esther 4:3 NIV).

"Your disciples do not fast?" (Matthew 9:14 NIV).

John the Baptist's disciples came to Jesus and asked him why his disciples did not fast as the Pharisees and John's disciples did. Jesus told them there was no need for them to fast as long as he was there; later, when he was gone, they would fast. (See Matthew 9:14-15.)

"I humbled my soul with fasting" (Psalm 35:13 KJV). Fasting is a way to deny our flesh; in our physical weakness we seek to grow stronger spiritually. Jesus gave some instructions on fasting and prayer in Matthew 6:5-18. We may also fast and pray to be more attuned to the leading of the Lord in a situation. The church in Antioch fasted and prayed before sending out Saul (Paul) and Barnabas to do the work of the Lord. (See Acts 13:2-3.)

Prayer: Father, when we fast and pray, please hear our cry for help and meet our needs. Amen

Day 151

"Many lay in sackcloth and ashes" (Esther 4:3 NIV).

"David and the elders of Israel, who were clothed in sackcloth, fell upon their faces" (1 Chronicles 21:16 KJV).

During great trouble or sorrow people in Bible times often clothed themselves in a coarse material called sackcloth and sat in ashes. This was a sign of humility and sorrow.

King David was enticed by Satan to have a count made of how many were in Israel's army. After the census, David realized he had sinned against God. God gave David three choices for his punishment: three years of famine, three months of being attacked by their enemies, or three days of the Lord's sword. David chose to suffer from the hand of God instead of the hand of their enemies because he knew God was merciful. The Lord sent a plague and seventy thousand men died. During this time, David and the elders were clothed in sackcloth. At God's command, David was to build an altar (on a man's property) and offer a burnt sacrifice, so the Lord would stop the plague. The owner wanted to give the land and the oxen for the offering to David, but David refused and paid him. David felt it would not be much of a sacrifice if it cost him nothing. (See 1 Chronicles 21.)

Prayer: Lord, may our lives be our sacrifice to you. Amen (See Romans 12:1.)

Day 152

"When Esther's eunuchs and female attendants came and told her about Mordecai, *she was in great distress*" (Esther 4:4 NIV).

"We must through much tribulation enter into the kingdom of God" (Acts 14:22 KJV).

There will be trials and struggles in the Christian life but we have the Lord to help us. Sometimes we don't understand what is happening or why, but if we hold on to him, he will carry us through. We shouldn't be surprised that we have to go through difficult times. If we read the Bible it is clear that trouble and trials come to all God's people.

It is true that we can be spared some troubles in life if we obey the Lord's commands; but there will be troubles even when we obey. Jesus told us not to fret about tomorrow's troubles because we have enough troubles today to keep us busy. (See Matthew 6:34.) Jesus faced many trials on earth and he was perfect.

Prayer: Lord, carry us through our trials in a way that gives glory to you. Amen

Day 153

"She sent clothes for [Mordecai] to put on instead of his sackcloth, but he would not accept them" (Esther 4:4 NIV).

"My clothing was sackcloth" (Psalm 35:13 KJV).

Esther didn't like to see Mordecai suffering; she tried to dress him up in normal clothing and pretend all was well. She didn't know why he was acting this way, but she planned to find out.

In Matthew 16, Jesus was telling his disciples that he would suffer and be killed and on the third day be raised to life. Peter didn't believe this and told Jesus so, rebuking him for such an absurd statement. Jesus in turn rebuked Peter, because he was being influenced by Satan. Peter couldn't believe anything terrible could happen to the Messiah. He and the other disciples wanted a conquering Messiah, not one that would be conquered (in their eyes).

There will be "sackcloth" times in our lives. Denying the circumstances will not help; we need to press in to God and hold fast to the promises in his Word.

Prayer: Thank you, Jesus, for doing the will of the Father even though it was very difficult. Help us in our hard times to rely on you. Amen

"Then Esther summoned Hathak, one of the king's eunuchs assigned to attend her, and ordered him to find out" (Esther 4:5 NIV).

"Call to me and I will answer you and tell you great and unsearchable things you do not know" (Jeremiah 33:3 NIV).

Esther wanted Hathak to find out what was going on with Mordecai.

Hathak and all of the eunuchs who care for Esther represent the Holy Spirit. We can call on the Holy Spirit to give us wisdom and knowledge about a situation that is troubling us. With that knowledge, we may be able to solve the problem, or trust that the Lord will work it out.

The Holy Spirit also reveals God's word to us so we can learn more about him. He can open up to us a verse or story in scripture we already know and we see it in a new way.

We are not alone; his Spirit will be with us forever. (See John 14:16.) As long as we follow Christ, we will have his Holy Spirit to be with us. The more we heed the promptings of the Spirit the clearer we will hear his voice. If we persist in being in control, and don't obey the voice of the Spirit, our own voice of reasoning will drown out the Spirit's voice.

"Today if [you] will hear his voice, harden not your hearts" (Hebrews 4:7 KJV).

Prayer: Thank you, Father, for sending your Holy Spirit to help us, may we heed his directions. Amen

Day 155

"What was troubling Mordecai and why" (Esther 4:5 NIV).

"My soul is overwhelmed with sorrow to the point of death" (Mark 14:34 NIV).

In Mark 14:32-36, Jesus is in the garden called Gethsemane with his disciples, when he pulls a few of them aside to come with him while he prays. He knows his time is short – he is soon to be arrested and crucified. He is deeply distressed and troubled—he is about to take on the sins of the whole world. He prayed to his Father that if it be possible, he would not have to go through with this. "And being in … agony he prayed more earnestly: and his sweat was as it were great drops of blood falling down to the ground" (Luke 22:44 KJV). Jesus prayed three times to be released from this responsibility; but he submitted to the Father's will and went to the cross.

Prayer: Jesus, thank you for enduring such agony for us. Amen

Day 156

"So Hathak went out to Mordecai in the open square of the city in front of the king's gate" (Esther 4:6 NIV).

When Jesus was baptized, "the heavens were opened ... and he saw the Spirit of God descending like a dove, and lighting upon him: And ... a voice from heaven, saying, This is my beloved Son, in whom I am well pleased" (Matthew 3:16-17 KJV).

We see the Trinity here: Jesus in the water, the Holy Spirit descending, and the Father speaking. Consider Esther 4:6 this way; Mordecai (Jesus) is in the open square, Hathak (Holy Spirit) went to him and he is at the king's (Father's) gate.

Jesus commanded his disciples to go and make other disciples of Jesus and for them to be baptized in the name of the Father, Son and Holy Spirit. (See Matthew 28:19.) Water baptism is an identification with Christ's death and resurrection. We are "buried" in the water then "rise" out of the water.

Baptism is also symbolic of dying to the old life we once lived and starting anew. "We are buried with him by baptism into death: that like as Christ was raised up from the dead by the glory of the Father, even so we also should walk in newness of life" (Romans 6:4 KJV). (See also Galatians 2:20.)

Prayer: Lord, water baptism is our public identification with you; may you be glorified. Amen

Day 157

"Mordecai told him everything that had happened to him" (Esther 4:7 NIV).

"And beginning at Moses and all the prophets, he expounded unto them in all the scriptures the things concerning himself" (Luke 24:27 KJV).

After Jesus' resurrection he joined up with two men walking to Emmaus; they did not recognize him. They told him about the terrible things that had happened recently concerning Jesus of Nazareth, a mighty prophet. Jesus scolds them for being so slow to believe the things the prophets spoke about. He begins to tell them the Old Testament prophecies about the Messiah (meaning himself). They urged him to come to their home because it was late in the day. He agreed and went with them.

When they sat down to eat he picked up the bread, gave thanks to God for it, and divided it among them. Their eyes were opened and they realized the stranger was Jesus. At that moment he disappeared. Immediately they left and found the eleven disciples and told them that they had seen Jesus.

Prayer: Jesus you are alive! Breathe life in us that we may live also. Amen

"Including the exact amount of money Haman had promised to pay into the royal treasury for the destruction of the Jews" (Esther 4:7 NIV).

"And [Judas] cast down the pieces of silver in the temple, …. And the chief priests took the silver pieces, and said, It is not lawful … to put them into the treasury, because it is the price of blood" (Matthew 27:5-6 KJV).

Jesus' disciple, Judas, was paid thirty pieces of silver from the temple treasury to hand Jesus over to the chief priests. After he betrayed Jesus, he felt convicted for what he had done and returned the thirty silver coins and went out and hanged himself. The chief priests could not put the money back into the temple treasury because it had been used to pay for someone to be murdered. Instead, they bought a field to bury strangers in. This was prophesied hundreds of years earlier in Zechariah 11:12-13.

Prayer: Jesus, if Judas had returned to you and had asked for forgiveness, you would have forgiven him. When we sin, may we turn to you and ask for forgiveness and be restored. Amen

Day 159

"He also gave him *a copy of the text of the edict for their annihilation,* which had been published in Susa" (Esther 4:8 NIV).

"The soul that [sins], it shall die" (Ezekiel 18:20 KJV).

The Bible is our copy of the edict and it tells us the penalty for sin is death:

God told Adam if he ate of the tree of the knowledge of good and evil, he would die. (Genesis 2:17)

Those who chase evil will die. (Proverbs 11:19)

People who hate correction will die. (Proverbs 15:10)

If you live to satisfy your fleshly sinful desires, you will die. (Romans 8:13)

Thank God that he provided an escape clause; through Jesus we can live:

Those who believe in Jesus shall have life forever. (John 3:36)

To know the true God and Jesus Christ his Son is life. (John 17:3)

If, by the Holy Spirit you destroy the wickedness within you, you shall live. (Romans 8:13)

Prayer: Lord, save us, we want to live. Amen

Day 160

"To show to Esther and explain it to her, and he told him to instruct her" (Esther 4:8 NIV).

"All scripture is given by inspiration of God, and is profitable for ... instruction in righteousness" (2 Timothy 3:16 KJV).

We have the Bible, God's word, for giving us instructions for the right way to live. In the Old Testament, we read how God gave the Israelites the Ten Commandments (see Exodus 20) and other laws to guide them in how they were to live their lives.

The Ten Commandments in condensed form:
1. You may not have other gods.
2. You may not make images and bow down to them or serve them.
3. You may not speak the name of the Lord in an unholy way.
4. Keep the Sabbath day holy and rest.
5. Honor your parents.
6.-10. You may not murder, commit adultery, steal, give false testimony or covet.

In the New Testament, Jesus summed up all the laws of God by saying; you should love God with all your heart and love others as yourself. (See Matthew 22:34-40.)

Prayer: Thank you, God, for the Bible that tells us how to live our lives in a way that pleases you. Amen

Day 161

"To go into the king's presence to beg for mercy" (Esther 4:8 NIV).

"Let us ... come boldly unto the throne of grace, that we may obtain mercy, and find grace to help in time of need" (Hebrews 4:16 KJV).

Christ paid the penalty for our sins on the cross. Because of Christ, all can go into the King's presence to beg for his mercy.

In the parable of the Pharisee and the tax collector, the Pharisee in his prayer thanked God he was not a big sinner like others he knew—for example the tax collector. He also boasted to God that he fasted and paid tithes. The tax collector humbly told God he knew he was a sinner; he asked for God to show him mercy. God heard and answered his prayer, but not the Pharisee's. God will humble the proud and lift up the humble. (See Luke 18:10-14.)

We can go boldly to the throne of God; but to be heard by him, we need to go humbly.

Prayer: Lord, may we come humbly before your throne and ask for mercy. Amen

Esther Chapter 4

Day 162

"And plead with him for her people" (Esther 4:8 NIV).

"Save us, O God of our salvation" (1 Chronicles 16:35 KJV).

Mordecai wanted Esther to go to the king on behalf of their people, the Jews, that they might be saved from the enemies who planned to kill them.

Paul said in Romans 10:1 (KJV): "Brethren, my heart's desire and prayer to God for Israel is, that they may be saved." Paul was praying that the Jews might know Jesus as their Messiah and Savior.

We can also go to the King of kings and plead for our people: our families, our friends, our country and our world. God is just as concerned about people today as he was in Bible times. His love is just as strong, his power is just as great, and his mercy is still available to those who ask.

Prayer: Lord, we pray for your Spirit to draw all people to you. Amen

Day 163

"And Hatach came and told Esther the words of Mordecai" (Esther 4:9 KJV).

The Spirit will come and tell the church the words of Jesus. (See John 16:13-15.)

Hathak was Mordecai's messenger to Esther just as the Holy Spirit is Jesus' messenger to the church. Jesus is not walking the earth in bodily form as he once did, but God sent us his Holy Spirit, instead.

In Acts 21:10-11 Agabus, a prophet, gave a word to Paul by the Holy Spirit warning him that the Jewish leaders in Jerusalem would arrest Paul and hand him over to the Gentile authorities. Earlier, (20:23) the Holy Spirit had told Paul that trials and imprisonment awaited him.

When the Holy Spirit speaks a word of instruction or direction to us, from the word of God or in our spirit, he often will have it confirmed by another person or confirmed by our circumstances. This conformation gives us a little more confidence in doing what we feel the Lord is leading us to do. The Holy Spirit will not lead us to do anything that contradicts the character of God or that doesn't line up with the Bible.

Prayer: Holy Spirit, lead us in the way of righteousness and direct our paths. Amen

Day 164

"Then she instructed him to say to Mordecai" (Esther 4:10 NIV).

"The Spirit ... [makes] intercession for the saints" (Romans 8:27 KJV).

The Spirit helps us to pray when we don't know how to pray. Sometimes we are just too crushed by the circumstances of life to pray audible or even coherent, silent words of prayer. That's when the Spirit steps in and prays for us. (See Romans 8:26.)

In times of distress or discouragement you may be helped by reading through the Psalms. Here are a few verses from Psalm 27:

"The LORD is my light and my salvation; whom shall I fear? the LORD is the strength of my life; of whom shall I be afraid?"

"For in the time of trouble he shall hide me in his pavilion."

"Hear, O LORD, when I cry with my voice: have mercy also upon me, and answer me."

"Wait on the LORD: be of good courage, and he shall strengthen [your] heart" (Psalm 27:1, 5, 7, 14 KJV).

Prayer: Lord, when we can't pray, please hear the cry of our hearts and answer. Amen

Day 165

"All the king's officials and the people of the royal provinces know that for *any man or woman who approaches the king in the inner court without being summoned the king has but one law: that they be put to death*" (Esther 4:11 NIV).

"The LORD said to Moses: 'Tell your brother Aaron that he is not to come whenever he chooses into the Most Holy Place behind the curtain … or else he will die" (Leviticus 16:2 NIV).

Aaron, the high priest, was not to go behind the dividing curtain in the tabernacle whenever he wanted. (Behind the curtain in the Most Holy Place is where God's presence resided.) God is a holy God and even the priest could not approach him except in the prescribed way and at certain times. To disobey meant death.

When Jesus died, God tore the dividing curtain of the temple in two (see Mark 15:38) to signify that now all could approach him by believing in the sacrifice of his son, Jesus. (See Ephesians 3:12.) Because of Christ we can approach a holy God anytime day or night.

Prayer: Thank you, God, that through faith in your Son we can approach you with confidence. Amen

Esther Chapter 4

"Unless the king extends the gold scepter to them and spares their lives" (Esther 4:11 NIV).

"The scepter shall not depart from Judah" and "There shall come a Star out of Jacob, and a Scepter shall rise out of Israel" (Genesis 49:10; Numbers 24:17 KJV).

These are Old Testament prophesies about Jesus. (A scepter represents authority. Possibly, a "gold" scepter represents the highest, most valuable authority.) Jesus is the gold scepter the Father has extended to us. If we believe, our lives are spared; we are no longer among the dead but among the living, for eternity. (See John 5:24.)

God is full of mercy and compassion. "It is of the Lord's mercies that we are not consumed, because his compassions fail not. They are new every morning: great is [your] faithfulness" (Lamentations 3:22-23 KJV). God in his mercy gave us his Son so that our lives would be spared an eternity of separation from his love and goodness.

Prayer: Thank you, Father, that you gave us your Son so that our lives are spared. Amen

Day 167

"But thirty days have passed since *I was called to go* to the king" (Esther 4:11 NIV).

"I was called to go …"

Name these people who were called to go.

I was called to go into the ark. (Genesis 7:1)

I was called to go to a land the Lord would show me. (Genesis 12:1)

I was called to go to Egypt so lives would be spared. (Genesis 45:5)

I was called to go to Egypt to bring the Israelites out. (Exodus 3:10)

I was called to go and lead God's people into the promised land. (Joshua 1:2)

I was called to go and prepare the way for the Messiah. (Matthew 3:3)

I was called to go to the lost sheep of the Israelites. (Matthew 15:24)

I was called to go to the Gentiles and tell them about Jesus. (Acts 9:15)

Where are you called to go?

Prayer: Lord, help us to go to where you call us to go. Amen

"And they told ... Mordecai Esther's words" (Esther 4:12 KJV).

"The LORD [has] heard my supplication; the LORD will receive my prayer" (Psalm 6:9 KJV).

Again, the Holy Spirit aids us in our prayers; our words are heard in heaven.

Here are some things to pray for:

Peace: "Pray for the peace of Jerusalem" (Psalm 122:6 KJV).

Repentance: "Repent, ... and turn to God, so that your sins may be wiped out" (Acts 3:19 NIV).

Authorities: May "prayers, intercessions, and giving of thanks, be made for all ... For kings, and for all that are in authority" (1 Timothy 2:1-2 KJV).

Yourself: "Hear me when I call, O God ... have mercy upon me, and hear my prayer" (Psalm 4:1 KJV).

Each Other: "Confess your faults one to another, and pray for one another" (James 5:16 KJV).

Revival in our country: "If my people, which are called by my name, shall humble themselves, and pray, and seek my face, and turn from their wicked ways; then will I hear from heaven, and will forgive their sin, and will heal their land" (2 Chronicles 7:14 KJV).

Prayer: Lord, we lift (the list above) to you. May you show mercy. Amen

Day 169

"He sent back this answer: 'Do not think that because you are in the king's house you alone of all the Jews will escape'" (Esther 4:13 NIV).

"How shall we escape, if we neglect so great salvation?" (Hebrews 2:3 KJV).

Don't think that just because you are in the King's house (a church building) you will escape.

Some people attend church as a social activity. Others feel they must or want to support a family tradition. Some may attend to find a mate or to receive the help or services a church may provide. Many churches have ministries in which people can volunteer to help in their community and that attracts some to the church. None of these reasons are wrong by themselves, if it is a first step toward the best reason to be going, which is to find God and commit their lives to him.

Attending church and being the Church are two different things. Going to church and participating in church activities does not save us; only a personal relationship with Jesus Christ. God has given us everything we need to escape his wrath; to believe in and obey his Son is all that is required.

Prayer: Lord, the building is not the church, your people are. So help us to be the Church that you desire us to be. Amen

"For if you remain silent at this time, relief and deliverance for the Jews will arise from another place, but you and your father's family will perish" (Esther 4:14 NIV).

"For if you remain silent at this time, [praise] will arise from another place."

"If they keep quiet, the stones will cry out" (Luke 19:40 NIV).

As Jesus was entering Jerusalem the people were loudly praising God. The Pharisees complained to him about this. Jesus told them that if they were to remain silent the stones would cry out in praise.

> Here are some verses about praise to God.
> "Great is the LORD, and greatly to be praised."
> "Daily shall he be praised."
> "I will praise [you], O Lord my God, with all my heart."
> "From the rising of the sun unto the going down of the same the LORD'S name is to be praised" (Psalm 48:1, 72:15, 86:12, 113:3 KJV).

Prayer: Lord, may all that have breath praise you. Amen (See Psalm 150:6.)

Day 171

"And who knows but that you have come to your royal position for such a time as this?" (Esther 4:14 NIV).

"Now is my soul troubled; and what shall I say? Father, save me from this hour: but for this cause [I came] unto this hour" (John 12:27 KJV).

Jesus came to do the will of the Father and that was to give his life for the fallen human race. Jesus had come to the earth "for such a time as this." No one could do this for him—he alone was the sinless man: the only one qualified and worthy to take our place, to take our punishment to satisfy a holy God.

"Who his own self bare our sins in his own body on the tree, that we, being dead to sins, should live unto righteousness" (1 Peter 2:24 KJV). He suffered so we could be righteous before God.

This is John's account of the crucifixion:

"And he bearing his cross went forth into a place called the place of a skull, which is called in the Hebrew Golgotha: Where they crucified him, and two [others] with him, on either side [was] one, and Jesus in the midst. And Pilate wrote a title, and put it on the cross. And the writing was, JESUS OF NAZARETH THE KING OF THE JEWS" (John 19:17-19 KJV).

Prayer: Jesus, thank you for dying a horrible death for us. Amen

"Then Esther sent this reply to Mordecai" (Esther 4:15 NIV).

Mary replied, "Be it unto me according to [your] word" (Luke 1:38 KJV).

The angel Gabriel appeared to Mary and told her she had been chosen to carry the Son of God. She humbly accepted the privilege and the responsibility. (See Luke 1:28-38.) This was Mary's "for such a time as this." Both Esther and Mary were given their assignment and they both carried it out to completion.

"For [you] are bought with a price: therefore glorify God in your body, and in your spirit, which are God's" (1 Corinthians 6:20 KJV). We are God's servants, bought by the blood of Christ. We are no longer our own but are to live as servants to him. Servants obey the voice of their master. If the master says come, they come; if he says go, they go; if he says do this, they do it. (See Matthew 8:9; Romans 1:1.)

We have assignments from God just as Esther, Mary and Jesus had theirs.

Prayer: Lord, you have given us each an assignment for this season in our lives; give us your wisdom and strength to carry it out, we pray. Amen

Day 173

"Go, gather together all the Jews who are in Susa, and fast for me. *Do not eat or drink for three days, night or day*" (Esther 4:16 NIV).

"For as [Jonah] was [fasting] three days and three nights in the whale's belly; so shall the Son of man be three days and three nights in the heart of the earth" (Matthew 12:40 KJV).

Jesus foretold his death using an Old Testament prophet as an example.

Jonah, a prophet of the Lord, was instructed by God to go the wicked city of Nineveh. Instead of obeying the Lord, he fled and boarded a ship headed to Tarshish. On the way, the Lord sent a violent storm. Jonah told those on the ship his story and suggested they throw him overboard because he was the cause of the storm. When the storm worsened, they saw no other way and threw him overboard. Then the sea calmed down. The sailors feared God and made vows to him. The Lord had a whale swallow Jonah and he was there three days and nights. He prayed to the Lord for help and God had the whale spit him out on dry ground.

The Lord spoke to Jonah a second time and told him to go to Nineveh. So Jonah went to Nineveh. He preached and the whole city turned to God. (See the Book of Jonah.)

Prayer: Lord, you have creative ways to get us to do your will; help us to obey quickly so your discipline is not needed to prompt us. Amen

Day 174

"I and my attendants will fast as you do" (Esther 4:16 NIV).
"When you fast" (Matthew 6:16 NIV).

In Matthew 6:16-18 Jesus talks to his disciples about fasting; he instructs them not to draw attention to themselves when they fast. Do not broadcast your fast and you will be rewarded by the Father. Our fasting is to get God's attention, not others; by fasting we are showing God that this request is important to us. Fasting is a way of humbling ourselves before God; we need him.

Here's more on the story of Jonah:

Jonah preached to the people of Nineveh and told them that God was going to overthrow their city. The people believed God. Then the king made a decree that everyone was to fast and put on sackcloth—even the animals; and to turn from their wicked ways and call on God. Perhaps he might show them mercy and spare the city. "And God saw their works, that they turned from their evil way" so he changed his mind and didn't let them be overthrown. (Jonah 3:10 KJV)

Prayer: Lord, when we fast and pray may you hear and answer our prayers. Amen

Day 175

"When this is done, I will go to the king, even though it is against the law. *'And if I perish, I perish'*" (Esther 4:16 NIV).

"Unless you repent, you too will all perish" (Luke 13:5 NIV).

Jesus asked those around him if they thought that the Galileans Pilate had killed were killed because they were worse sinners than others. Then he brought up the tragedy of a tower in Siloam that fell on eighteen people and killed them. Were they more wicked than others who were spared? No! he told them; but if they didn't turn to God they would perish as well. (See Luke 13:1-5.)

"For God so loved the world, that he gave his only ... Son, that whosoever [believes] in him should not perish, but have everlasting life. For God sent not his Son into the world to condemn the world; but that the world through him might be saved" (John 3:16-17 KJV). The one who believes in Jesus and turns from sin will not perish.

Prayer: Lord, may we believe and follow you so that we do not perish. Amen

"So Mordecai went away" (Esther 4:17 NIV).
"I am going away" (John 16:7 NIV).

Jesus told his disciples that he was going away. He came from the Father in heaven to the world and he would soon leave this world and return to the Father. He tried to prepare his disciples for his departure, and to comfort them by promising them the Holy Spirit.

He also told them the time was coming when they would scatter and leave him alone; but he wouldn't be totally alone because the Father would be with him.

He would soon be gone, then be back for a little while, then gone again—to be with his Father. He said they would weep and be sorrowful, but only for a short time; then they would have great joy. (He was talking about his death and resurrection.) (See John 16.)

Prayer: Jesus, you went away, but you are coming back again. Thank you that you keep your promises. Amen

Day 177

"And carried out all of Esther's instructions" (Esther 4:17 NIV).

"And this is the confidence that we have in him, that, if we ask [anything] according to his will, he [hears] us: And if we know that he [hears] us, whatsoever we ask, we know that we have the petitions that we desired of him" (1 John 5:14-15 KJV).

Pray throughout your day:

P- Pray and keep on praying. Pray in faith and don't give up. (Luke 18:1)

R- Reach toward what is ahead, forget the past and move on. (Philippians 3:13)

A-Acknowledge him in all your ways and he will guide you. (Proverbs 3:6)

Y- Yoke up with him, he will help you carry the weight. (Matthew 11:29)

E- Endure hardship; it's the Father's discipline for you. (Hebrews 12:7)

R- Rest in God after you have prayed your heart out to him. (Psalm 62:5, 8)

Prayer: Thank you, God, that you hear our prayers. Amen

Chapter 4 Review

Day 150: Fasting is a way to deny our flesh.

Day 156: Water baptism symbolizes dying to the old life we once lived and starting anew.

Day 163: The Holy Spirit will not lead us to do anything that contradicts the character of God or that doesn't line up with the Bible.

Day 164: Sometimes we are just too crushed by the circumstances of life to pray. That's when the Spirit steps in and prays for us.

Day 167: Where are you called to go?

Day 176: Jesus, you went away but you are coming back again.

Day 177: Pray and keep on praying. Pray in faith and don't give up.

Day 177: Rest in God after you have prayed your heart out.

Prayer: Lord, help us to pray and not give up. Amen

Day 179

Chapter 4 Challenge

Answer the questions below.

1. When Mordecai and the other Jews heard about the edict, what did they do? (4:1-3)

2. Who told Esther about Mordecai's behavior? (4:4)

3. What did she do for Mordecai? (4:4)

4. What did Mordecai send to Esther? And what did he ask of her? (4:8)

5. What answer did she send back to Mordecai? (4:11)

6. How many days had it been since she had seen the king? (4:11)

7. For how many days did she ask the Jews to fast for her? (4:16)

8. What was her fateful reply? (4:16)

Prayer: Father, help us when we have to do hard things. Amen

Day 180

"On the third day" (Esther 5:1 NIV).

"On the third day he will be raised to life!" (Matthew 20:19 NIV).

In Genesis 22, the Lord told Abraham to take his son Isaac, whom he greatly loved, and offer him as a burnt offering. The next morning, they set out. On the third day, Abraham saw the place where God wanted him to make the sacrifice. Abraham tied up Isaac and put him on the altar. He was about to kill his son when an angel called out to him. God saw that Abraham was willing to offer his son in obedience to him. God provided a ram for him to offer instead. Isaac, in a sense, was raised to life! This is what happened on the third day. (This was a type of God and his Son.)

Jesus and his disciples went to Jerusalem. Days later, he was arrested and taken to the chief priests who demanded his death. He was handed over to the Gentile rulers, who had him beaten, mocked and crucified. Three days later, Mary Magdalene saw that the tomb was empty. Jesus was raised to life! This is what happened on the third day. (See Matthew 21, 26-28.)

You may be going through a difficult time or season of life. Just be patient and remember what happens on the third day!

Prayer: Lord, we are trusting you to raise us up on the third day! Amen

Day 181

"Esther put on her royal robes" (Esther 5:1 NIV).

"For he [has] clothed me with the garments of salvation, he [has] covered me with the robe of righteousness" (Isaiah 61:10 KJV).

Since we are God's people, we should dress in the type of royal clothing he wears: mercy, kindness and patience. (See Colossians 3:12.) By yielding to the Holy Spirit within us, we are clothed with these qualities that please the Lord. The Bible also uses the term "fruit" as the outward evidence of the holiness within. Just as we know a peach tree because it has peaches on it, Jesus said that we could recognize true believers by their fruit. A good tree produces good fruit and a bad tree produces bad fruit. (See Matthew 7:15-20.)

As followers of Christ, we have his Spirit in us; but we should allow the Spirit to flow out of us. When we do, the character of Christ is exhibited in our everyday circumstances and others see our royal robes of holy living.

Prayer: Lord, may we yield to you so that our spiritual clothing reflects the good God that we serve. Amen

Esther Chapter 5

"And stood in the inner court of the palace, in front of the king's hall" (Esther 5:1 NIV).

"We have confidence to enter the Most Holy Place by the blood of Jesus, by a new and living way opened for us through the curtain, that is, his body" (Hebrews 10:19-20 NIV).

"I looked, and, behold, a door was opened in heaven" the Apostle John said in relating his vision in Revelation 4:1 (KJV). A door of access has been opened to us through the sacrifice of God's son. As believers, we can enter into the very throne room of God with confidence because Jesus' blood has cleansed us from our sins. What was once forbidden—approaching God in the holy place behind the curtain—now is allowed; we can freely come before God.

"Come now, and let us reason together, [says] the LORD: though your sins be as scarlet, they shall be as white as snow; though they be red like crimson, they shall be as wool" (Isaiah 1:18 KJV).

Prayer: Thank you, Jesus, for making a way for us to come boldly before the Father. Amen

Day 183

"The king was sitting on his royal throne in the hall, facing the entrance" (Esther 5:1 NIV).

"I saw the LORD sitting on his throne, and all the hosts of heaven standing by him on his right hand and on his left" (1 Kings 22:19 KJV).

The Lord is sitting on his throne:

Isaiah said, "In the year that king Uzziah died I saw also the Lord sitting upon a throne, high and lifted up, and his train filled the temple" (Isaiah 6:1 KJV).

The prophet Daniel saw in a vision a throne where God, called the Ancient of Days, sat. His "garment was white as snow, and the hair of his head like the pure wool: his throne was like the fiery flame and his wheels as burning fire" (Daniel 7:9 KJV).

The Apostle John in the Spirit saw someone sitting on the throne in heaven and there was a rainbow around the throne and lightning and thunder. "And before the throne there was a sea of glass like unto crystal: and in the midst of the throne and round about the throne, were four beasts full of eyes before and behind" (Revelation 4:6 KJV).

Prayer: God, you are on your throne now and forever; your kingdom does not end. Amen

"When he saw Queen Esther standing in the court, he was pleased with her and held out to her the gold scepter that was in his hand" (Esther 5:2 NIV).

"For the Lord [takes] pleasure in his people" (Psalm 149:4 KJV).

God is pleased when we come to him in the prescribed way—through his Son. He is pleased when we follow his ways and obey his commands, just as an earthly father would be.

The Lord created everything for his own pleasure. He is worthy of honor and praise. (See Revelation 4:11.) We were made for him. He wants a relationship with us; because he made us, he knows best how to make that relationship work. He loves us and wants us to love him back. He wants us to trust him and look to him as our loving but wise Father. He sometimes leads us where we don't want to go, but he promises to go with us. One day we will be united with him forever.

Prayer: Father, may we give you pleasure today by loving you. Amen

Day 185

"So Esther approached and touched the tip of the scepter" (Esther 5:2 NIV).

"A woman … with an issue … came … and touched the hem of his garment" (Matthew 9:20 KJV).

Esther had an issue for which she needed to go to the king. All of us have issues that trouble us.

This woman, with an issue, who also is mentioned in the Gospel of Mark, had spent all that she had going to doctors but she only grew worse. When she heard about Jesus, she believed that if she could touch even his clothes she would be made well. She did touch his garment and was healed. Her issue was taken care of. (See Mark 5:25-34.)

We may also go to Jesus with the issues that afflict us day after day, year after year. This woman had suffered with this for twelve years. Jesus said he would never send anyone away who came to him. (See John 6:37.) He may or may not deliver us (in this life) from the trouble we are having, but he will certainly be with us and help us through it, if we ask him and put our trust in him.

Prayer: Father, may we give you the issues in our lives and may you help us. Amen

"Then the king asked, *'What is it,* Queen Esther?'" (Esther 5:3 NIV).

The Israelites asked, "What is it?" (Exodus 16:15 NIV).

The Israelites asked this question while they were in the wilderness. Moses answered, "This is the bread which the Lord [has] given you to eat" (Exodus 16:15 KJV). They called it manna. The Lord provided this bread for them for forty years. This bread was symbolic of the bread he would later send for all the people of the world, his Son.

Jesus said "I am the living bread which came down from heaven: if any man eat of this bread, he shall live for ever" and "This is that bread which came down from heaven: not as your fathers did eat manna, and are dead: he that [eats] of this bread shall live for ever" (John 6:51, 58 KJV).

Jesus is the bread of life. He is the one who sustains us now and forever.

Prayer: Lord, you are the bread of life for our souls. Amen

Day 187

"What is your request?" (Esther 5:3 NIV).

"What do you want me to do for you?" (Mark 10:51 NIV).

Jesus once asked a blind man what he could do for him. The blind man said he wanted to see. Jesus told him to go on his way—his faith had healed him. (See Mark 10:51-52.) It was probably obvious to Jesus and the others that this man was blind, but Jesus still asked him what he could do for him. Jesus wants us to tell him what we need even though he already knows.

In Revelation 3:17-18 the church in Laodicea is proud of the fact that they are rich and don't need a thing. But they didn't realize that they were poor and blind (spiritually). The Lord advised them to buy from him gold refined in the fire so they could be rich (spiritually) and he would give them salve for their eyes so they could see (spiritually).

Our wealth in the physical world doesn't gain us favor in the spiritual realm.

Prayer: Lord, may we be spiritually rich and share those riches with others. Amen

"Even up to half the kingdom, it will be given you" (Esther 5:3 NIV).

"Unto you it has been given to know the mysteries of the kingdom of God" (Luke 8:10 KJV).

Jesus spoke often about his Father's kingdom:

The kingdom of heaven is like a farmer who planted good seed in his field. But during the night when the farmer and his farmhands were sleeping his enemy planted weeds in the field. Later, when the crops started to grow the helpers asked the farmer if he had planted good seed or not. There were weeds everywhere among the wheat. The farmer told them that his enemy had done that. The farmhands asked him if they should pull up the weeds and he said no, because that might uproot the wheat. At harvest time they could pull up the weeds and burn them; they would put the wheat in the barn.

God planted a good crop (the believers) but Satan came and planted weeds (the wicked). In the future, the angels of God will separate the good from the bad. The good will go to the Father and the bad will be burned. (See Matthew 13:24-30, 37-40.)

Prayer: Father, thank you that reveal the mysteries of your kingdom. Amen

Day 189

"'If it pleases the king,' replied Esther" (Esther 5:4 NIV).
"If it pleases the king" (Nehemiah 2:5 NIV).

Nehemiah worked for a king in a foreign land. When he heard how bad things were back in his home country and in Jerusalem, he wept. For quite a few days he fasted and prayed. In his prayer he confessed his sins and the sins of all the Israelites who had not obeyed the Lord's commands. The Lord had told them that if they didn't obey him, he would scatter them among the nations and that's what had happened. Nehemiah prayed and asked God for favor with the king.

The king noticed that Nehemiah was sad and he asked him why. So Nehemiah told him. The king asked him what he wanted. Nehemiah prayed, then gave him an answer. He said that if it pleased the king, he would like to go to Jerusalem to rebuild the city. The king gave him permission and even sent officers from the army to accompany him to see that he arrived safely. After they started rebuilding the walls of Jerusalem, their enemies tried to stop them. But the Lord was with them and the wall was rebuilt in record time—fifty-two days! (See Nehemiah 1-6.)

Prayer: God, you are a God of miracles. With you all things are possible. Amen

Esther Chapter 5

"Let the king, together with Haman, come today to a banquet I have prepared for him" (Esther 5:4 NIV).

"You prepare a table before me in the presence of my enemies" (Psalm 23:5 NIV).

Esther prepared a banquet and invited her enemy Haman.

The Bible says we are to give food and drink to our enemies; in doing this, we are showing them the love of Jesus. In inviting Haman, Esther was doing good to the one who intended evil for the Jews, her people. We do not overcome evil with evil. Instead we conquer evil by doing good. (See Romans 12:20-21.)

The prophet Elisha led his enemies to Samaria. The king of Israel asked him if they should be killed. Elisha said don't kill them but feed them. So the king had a banquet prepared for them; and after eating, they were sent home. And the enemies stopped raiding the Israelites' land. (See 2 Kings 6:19-23.)

Prayer: Lord, help us to show love to our enemies. Amen

Day 191

"'Bring Haman at once,' the king said, *so that we may do what Esther asks*'" (Esther 5:5 NIV).

"If any of you lack wisdom, ... [ask God], ... and it shall be given [to you]" (James 1:5 KJV).

When we ask God for wisdom, he gives it to us, but usually only a piece at a time or a step at a time. When we walk in a dense fog, we may see only two feet ahead; but as we move forward, we see the next two feet ahead, then the next.

When David's son Solomon was king; the Lord appeared to him in a dream and asked what he could give him. Solomon answered by asking for wisdom. God gave Solomon wisdom, greater than any person in the world. He became famous for his wisdom and kings from other nations sent representatives to hear him speak. (See 1 Kings 3:5-12.)

Jesus mentioned Solomon when he was talking about how the Lord made the flowers beautiful. He said that not even Solomon in his royal apparel could compete with them.

Another time he brought up Solomon, saying, a queen came from a long distance to see him and to hear his wisdom but now someone even greater than Solomon was here—referring to himself. (See Matthew 6:29, 12:42.)

Prayer: Lord, you are the wise one—there is no one like you. Amen

Esther Chapter 5

Day 192

"So the king and Haman went to the banquet Esther had prepared" (Esther 5:5 NIV).

"See, I have set before [you] this day life and good, and death and evil. ... choose life" (Deuteronomy 30:15, 19 KJV).

Each day we have a banquet of choices to feast on. Do we choose "life" represented by the king (God) or "death" represented by Haman (Satan)?

Adam and Eve had two sons, Cain and Abel. Abel raised flocks and Cain farmed the ground. Cain brought an offering to the Lord from his harvest. Abel brought an offering to the Lord from his flock. The Lord was pleased with Abel's offering but not with Cain's. This made Cain angry. The Lord told Cain that if he gave the proper offering it would be accepted. But if he didn't do what was right, he would be tempted to sin. Cain made a choice but a wrong one. He suggested to Abel that they walk out in the field. There Cain killed Abel his brother. The Lord confronted Cain with his sin and put him under a curse and caused him to be a nomad on the earth. (See Genesis 4.)

Prayer: Lord, help us to make right choices today. May we choose life. Amen

Day 193

"As they were drinking wine" (Esther 5:6 NIV).

"And be not drunk with wine ... but be filled with the Spirit" (Ephesians 5:18 KJV).

In Acts 2, on the day of Pentecost, the Holy Spirit was poured out on the disciples and they spoke languages that they had not learned. When the people from other territories heard this, they were amazed that these local men were talking their languages. Some made fun of them and said they were drunk on wine. Peter stood up and said that they were not drunk, but this was a fulfillment of the prophecy in Joel. (See Joel 2:28-29.)

In this prophesy, the Lord promised to pour out his Spirit on all who believed in him and they would prophesy and have God-given dreams and visions. Peter went on to preach a sermon about Jesus. The people were convicted of their sins; they asked him what they needed to do to get right with God. Peter told them to turn from their sins and be baptized and they would be forgiven and then they could also receive the Holy Spirit.

Prayer: Father, fill us with your Holy Spirit. Amen

Day 194

"The king again asked Esther, 'Now what is your petition?'" (Esther 5:6 NIV).

"Do not be anxious about anything, but in every situation, by prayer and petition, with thanksgiving, present your requests to God" (Philippians 4:6 NIV).

The Lord wants to hear our petitions. He doesn't want us to worry about things but to ask for what we need—to leave the situation with him and thank him for the answer.

If you look into the lives of the Old Testament people, you will see that they sometimes had to wait for years, even decades, to receive an answer to their prayers.

In Luke 18:1-8, Jesus told his disciples a parable about being persistent in prayer. In this story a widow kept going to the judge for justice. He refused her for a time but then eventually gave in and gave her justice because of her persistence.

We serve a "slow cooker" God in a "microwave" world.

Prayer: Lord, help us not to get discouraged and stop praying but to continue until you answer. Amen

Day 195

"It will be given you" (Esther 5:6 NIV).

"Ask, and it shall be given you" (Matthew 7:7 KJV).

If we ask, we will receive, seek and we will find, knock and the door will open. All of these things—receiving, finding and the door opening—require us to do something first: ask, seek and knock. Prayer is active; we are involved in the process from the beginning to its completion—it's all done in faith.

"Give, and it shall be given unto you" (Luke 6:38 KJV).

This verse goes on to say whatever measure we use when we give, that amount is given back to us. When Jesus saw the poor widow put two small coins in the temple treasury, he said she put in more than everyone else. She put in all she had; others only put in of their surplus. (See Luke 21:1-4.)

"Speak: for it shall be given you" (Matthew 10:19 KJV).

Let's take the initiative and speak out in faith; when we do, we will be given the words needed. Verse 20 says we can do this because it's not really us speaking but the Holy Spirit speaking through us.

Prayer: Lord, as we ask, give and speak; may your will be done. Amen

"And what is your request?" (Esther 5:6 NIV).

"Let your requests be made known unto God" (Philippians 4:6 KJV).

Requests, not demands; God is in charge. "Do not be quick with your mouth ... God is in heaven and you are on earth, so let your words be few.... Do not let your mouth lead you into sin" (Ecclesiastes 5:2, 6 NIV).

Jephthah made a vow to the Lord saying that if the Lord gave him victory in battle, then he would sacrifice to the Lord whatever came out of his house first. (He was probably thinking of a lamb for the sacrifice.) The Lord did give him victory over the enemy. When he returned home the first out of his house was his only child—his daughter. He was devastated, but kept his vow to the Lord. (See Judges 11.)

If you make a vow to God keep it. But better yet, don't make a vow if you don't plan to honor it. (See Ecclesiastes 5:4-5.)

Prayer: Lord, may we not make vows quickly or take them lightly. Amen

Day 197

"Even up to half the kingdom, it will be granted" (Esther 5:6 NIV).

"Come, [you] blessed of my Father, inherit the kingdom prepared for you from the foundation of the world" (Matthew 25:34 KJV).

Here are two more parables about the kingdom:

The kingdom of God is like a small seed that grows and becomes a large plant. This plant provides shade for the birds. (See Mark 4:30-32.) When we first come to Christ, we are like a small seed but as we grow and become more Christ-like, we can be a source of comfort (shade) for others.

The kingdom of heaven is like a fishing net that was tossed into the sea and caught all kinds of fish. Then it was pulled up and taken to land. The fishermen sat down on the beach to sort the fish. They kept the good ones but threw the bad ones away. When the end comes, the angels of God will separate the evil from the good; the evil people will be cast into the furnace. (See Matthew 13:47-50.)

Prayer: Lord, thank you for telling us about your kingdom; we want to be a part of it. Amen

"Then answered Esther, and said, *My petition and my request is*" (Esther 5:7 KJV).

"And the king granted him all his request" (Ezra 7:6 KJV).

The Jewish exiles had returned to Jerusalem and the temple had been rebuilt and the religious celebrations were in full swing again. Then Ezra arrived from Babylon to be a spiritual leader to the people. He was a priest and a teacher of the Law of God and he obeyed the Lord's commands. He found favor with the king and the king gave him everything he had asked him for because God was with him.

It is good for us to have spiritual leaders that we can look up to—leaders that study the Bible and obey the Lord. It is a blessing to have pastors and teachers that teach the word of God as they are prompted by the Holy Spirit. That is one benefit of being part of the church, the body of Christ and being in his family; we can be fed corporately from God's word.

As we learn more from his Word, we can pray our requests more intelligently, because we now know better what things please God.

Prayer: Lord, as the king granted Ezra what he requested, may our requests to the King of kings be worth granting.

Day 199

"If I have found [favor] in the sight of the king" (Esther 5:8 KJV).

"I know that you are pleased with me, for my enemy does not triumph over me" (Psalm 41:11 NIV).

Elisha, a prophet of the Lord, was in Dothan one night when his enemies found him. They surrounded the city with horses and chariots. When Elisha and his servant got up in the morning, they saw the army and the servant was afraid. Elisha told him not to be afraid because the army on their side was bigger than the army he saw surrounding the city. Then Elisha prayed that the Lord would open the eyes of the servant so he would see the Lord's army. The Lord showed the servant his army—horses and chariots of fire all around Elisha. (See 2 Kings 6:13-17.)

"Greater is he that is in you, than he that is in the world" (1 John 4:4 KJV).

Prayer: Thank you, God, that you are greater than any enemy that comes against us. Amen

Day 200

"And if it please the king to grant my petition, and to perform my request" (Esther 5:8 KJV).

"Take delight in the LORD, and he will give you the desires of your heart" (Psalm 37:4 NIV).

As we make the Lord our delight, he will purify the desires of our heart. More and more as we draw closer to him his desires become our desires. As we pray more in keeping with his will, he answers and his purposes are accomplished. Most likely our prayers will not be answered in the way we thought he would answer, but his way is best.

There are many verses in the Bible that can be prayed, find scriptures to pray that are meaningful to you.

Prayer: "Create in me a clean heart, O God; and renew a right spirit within me. Cast me not away from [your] presence; and take not [your] holy spirit from me. Restore unto me the joy of [your] salvation" (Psalm 51:10-12 KJV). Amen

Day 201

"Let the king and Haman come to the banquet that I shall prepare for them, and I will do [tomorrow] as the king [has] said" (Esther 5:8 KJV).

"Do not say to your neighbor, 'Come back tomorrow and I'll give it to you—when you already have it with you'" (Proverbs 3:28 NIV).

Was Esther stalling for time?

It's easy to put things off until tomorrow, especially unpleasant tasks. But the sooner we take care of those unpleasant tasks, the better we feel, and the more we can enjoy the other responsibilities that are before us.

"Obey what I command you today" (Exodus 34:11 NIV). If we do today what the Lord says, then tomorrow we will have only tomorrow's assignments to do; not today's and tomorrow's. Jesus said today would give us enough to deal with. (See Matthew 6:34.)

Prayer: Lord, help us to do what we need to do today and trust you with tomorrow. Amen

"Haman went out that day happy and in high spirits" (Esther 5:9 NIV).

"Wine that [makes] glad the heart of man" (Psalm 104:15 KJV). (Verses 6 mentions they were drinking wine.)

Many are seeking something to make them happy and provide them with a high. People use whatever they can to dull the pain in life: drugs, alcohol, cigarettes, entertainment, shopping, food, people, and the list goes on.

God wants us to take refuge in him and not in these other things. "God is our refuge and strength, a very present help in trouble" (Psalm 46:1 KJV). When you are feeling down call out to God, put your hope in him and thank him for the things he has already done for you. (See Psalm 42.)

An ordinary thing can become our god when it becomes our main source of happiness or pain reliever in life. The Lord wants to be our main source of joy, and the pain reliever for our souls. If we ask him, God will show us the path of life; it's in his presence we find joy and pleasures forever. (See Psalm 16:11.)

"Trust in him at all times; … people, pour out your heart [and hurt] before him: God is a refuge for us" (Psalm 62:8 KJV).

Prayer: Lord, forgive us for making things our gods. Deliver us, that you may be our one and only God, and our source of life and healing. Amen

Day 203

"But when he saw Mordecai at the king's gate" (Esther 5:9 NIV).

"Enter through the narrow gate" (Matthew 7:13 NIV).

Jesus is the narrow gate. "Neither is there salvation in any other: for there is none other name under heaven given among men, whereby we must be saved" (Acts 4:12 KJV). There are no other roads to God; it is only through his son, Jesus.

Jesus said, "Strive to enter in at the [narrow] gate: for many, I say unto you, will seek to enter in, and shall not be able" (Luke 13:24 KJV). He went on to say that once the owner of the house has gotten up and shut the door there will be people left outside. They may knock on the door and ask to come in but the owner will say he doesn't know them. He tells them to leave—they are wicked. Then they will weep when they see the prophets of old in the kingdom of God; but they are shut out. (See Luke 13:25-28.)

Prayer: Lord, may those who don't know you call out to you before the door is shut and it is too late to enter. Amen

"And observed that he neither rose nor showed fear in his presence" (Esther 5:9 NIV).

"Only fear the LORD" (1 Samuel 12:24 KJV).

Jesus said for us not to be afraid of those who may kill us; they can only kill our bodies. He told us to fear God, because he has the power to destroy both soul and body in hell. (See Matthew 10:28.) Fear of God is a reverence for him and respect for his authority over everything.

"Blessed are all who fear the LORD, who walk in obedience to him" (Psalm 128:1 NIV).

He is the reason everything exists. He has the power and authority to create and to destroy. His almighty power is not out of control, but is restrained by his love and compassion for us.

Mordecai knew whom he should fear—God, not Haman or any person.

Prayer: Lord, may we love and fear you—you are worthy. Amen

Day 205

"[Haman] was filled with rage against Mordecai" (Esther 5:9 NIV).

"[The devil] is filled with fury, because he knows that his time is short" (Revelation 12:12 NIV).

The devil hates Christ and wages war against his church, but only for a time; then he will be judged and thrown into the lake of fire.

In Revelation12:9, the enemy of our souls is called a dragon, a serpent, the devil and Satan. Here are some different names given to the devil and opposite names given to God.

Devil	God
Thief (John 10:10)	Provider (Philippians 4:19)
Deceiver (Revelation 12:9)	Truth (John 14:6)
Adversary (1 Peter 5:8)	Friend (John 15:14)
Evil (Ephesians 6:16)	Good (Psalm 100:5)
Tempter (Matthew 4:3)	Peace (John 14:27)

Prayer: Lord, you are greater than the enemy—whatever name he's called. Amen

"Nevertheless, *Haman restrained himself and went home*" (Esther 5:10 NIV).

"Then the devil [left] him" (Matthew 4:11 KJV).

After Jesus was baptized in water by John, the Holy Spirit descended on him. The Spirit then led him into the desert, where he was tempted by the devil. He had been fasting for forty days and nights and he was very hungry.

The devil urged him to turn the stones around him into bread to eat. Jesus told him it is written in God's word that man needs more than bread to live, he needs the word of God.

Then the devil took him to the top of the temple and said if he was God's son to jump off and the angels would catch him. Jesus replied to the devil that God's word says we are not to test the power of God.

Next the devil put him on a mountain and showed him all the countries of the world. He promised them to Jesus if he would worship him as his god. Jesus quoted the Scriptures again and told him that worship belonged to the Lord God only.

Luke 4:13 (KJV) says, "And when the devil had ended all the temptation, he departed from him for a season."

Prayer: Thank you, Jesus, for resisting the temptations of the devil. Amen

Day 207

"Calling together his friends and Zeresh, his wife" (Esther 5:10 NIV).

"That day Herod and Pilate became friends—before this they had been enemies" (Luke 23:12 NIV).

After Jesus had been arrested, the next day both Herod and Pilate questioned Jesus. Later that same day Pilate handed Jesus over to be crucified. How easily enemies can become friends when they encounter a common enemy.

The Church could learn from this: instead of fighting among ourselves, we should join together in fighting the true enemy—Satan. In John 17:21-22, Jesus prayed to the Father that the church would be one (in agreement) as he and the Father were one, so that the world would believe in him. What a witness to the world it would be today if different church denominations worked together to advance the kingdom of God on the earth.

Prayer: Lord, may your Church unite for the sake of your kingdom. Amen

"Haman boasted to them about his vast wealth, his many sons, and all the ways the king had honored him and how he had elevated him above the other nobles and officials" (Esther 5:11 NIV).

"[There are those] that trust in their wealth, and boast ... of their riches." How futile for people to amass great riches for they will "perish, and leave their wealth to others" (Psalm 49:6, 10 KJV).

Jesus said it was hard for the rich to get into the kingdom of heaven. To enter the kingdom of God the rich must realize that they are poor without Christ. He is the true riches. Our trust needs to be in Christ, not in our wealth.

Jesus didn't have a lot of earthly possessions. He must not have owned a house since he said he didn't have a place to sleep. He apparently didn't have a horse or donkey to ride because he walked everywhere. The only time Scripture records him riding is on the way to Jerusalem; he rode a donkey that was borrowed. He even walked on the water— he didn't have a boat. (See Matthew 8:20, 14:25; Luke 19:30-35.)

In Jeremiah 9:23-24, the Lord says we are not to brag about our wisdom, strength or riches, but if we want something to brag about, let it be that we know the Lord. He is the one who is loving and kind, and does right toward everyone on the earth.

Prayer: Lord, may we put our hope and trust in you and not in money or wealth. Amen

Day 209

"[Haman's] many sons" (Esther 5:11 NIV).

"For wide is the gate, and broad is the way, that [leads] to destruction" and many are going that way. (Matthew 7:13 KJV)

Satan, like Haman, has many sons or followers. Sadly, some of these were once followers of Christ. Jesus encountered this problem after a hard teaching he gave: "From that time many of his disciples went back, and walked no more with him" (John 6:66 KJV).

Jesus also warned his disciples that in the last days many will leave the faith because of the evil in the world. But those who remain faithful to him will be saved eternally. (See Matthew 24:12-13.)

The easy way leads to destruction and many are headed there. It takes the power of God and our determined will to choose the narrow, difficult way, but that way has eternal value.

Prayer: Lord, wake up those who are headed to destruction that they may turn to you. Amen

Day 210

"'And that's not all,' Haman added. 'I'm the only person Queen Esther invited to accompany the king to the banquet she gave'" (Esther 5:12 NIV).

"Pride [goes] before destruction, and an haughty spirit before a fall" (Proverbs 16:18 KJV).

Haman is boasting about being an honored guest at Esther's feast. What he doesn't know is that his attendance is for the purpose of exposing his wickedness.

Uzziah was made king in Judah when he was sixteen years old. He followed the Lord under the direction of Zechariah. "And as long as he sought the LORD, God made him to prosper" (2 Chronicles 26:5 KJV). He rebuilt towns, built towers and had a powerful army. He became famous, but his pride led him to perform priestly duties, which he was not allowed to do. The Lord afflicted him with leprosy because of this great sin.

God detests pride. Pride was Satan's downfall.

Prayer: Lord, deliver us from pride and help us to walk humbly before you. Amen

Day 211

"And she has invited me along with the king tomorrow" (Esther 5:12 NIV).

"Do not boast about tomorrow, for you do not know what a day may bring" (Proverbs 27:1 NIV).

We shouldn't brag about what we will do tomorrow or in the future, we don't know how things will play out. Nor should we, like a soldier, boast of our greatness in battle when all we have done is dress in our uniform. (See 1 Kings 20:11.) We need to humbly commit our plans to the Lord and leave the results to him.

Peter had a hard lesson to learn.

Jesus told his disciples that they all would desert him. Peter claimed that even if all the others abandoned him, he wouldn't. Jesus told Peter that he would deny him three times that very night. Peter said he wouldn't—he was even ready to die with him. The other disciples agreed they would die with him, too. Later that night, Jesus was arrested and all the disciples scattered. Peter returned to watch what would happen to Jesus; and while there, when put to the test, he denied him three times just as Jesus predicted. (See Mark 14:27-72.)

Prayer: Lord, we can only stand if you hold us up; please hold us tight. Amen

"But all this gives me no satisfaction" (Esther 5:13 NIV).

"Death and destruction are never satisfied" (Proverbs 27:20 NIV).

Evil never cries, "Enough!" The devil is never satisfied with the havoc he creates; he is always planning more. Don't think that if you try to keep a low profile that he won't bother with you. He's had centuries to figure out the best tactics and plans to try to trip people up. If he isn't making much progress with you then he will go after your family. He plays dirty, but that's the only way he knows how to play.

So, go ahead, take the kingdom of God by storm. Be all in, go all out, be prayed up and get down to business with God. You only have a limited time here, so give it all you've got.

Prayer: God, may we make you the reason for living and give you our all. Amen

Day 213

"As long as I see that Jew Mordecai sitting at the king's gate" (Esther 5:13 NIV).

Christ is seated at the right hand of God and he is praying for us. (See Romans 8:34.)

Jesus is always "sitting at the king's gate" always on duty, going to the Father on our behalf. Jesus didn't forget about us after he returned to heaven. He is able to save all who call on God and believe in him because he is always praying for them. (See Hebrews 7:25.) "Our help is in the name of the LORD, who made heaven and earth" (Psalm 124:8 KJV).

Nothing can separate us from Christ's love—not even death.

"For I am persuaded, that neither death, nor life, nor angels, nor principalities, nor powers, nor things present, nor things to come, Nor height, nor depth, nor any other creature, shall be able to separate us from the love of God, which is in Christ Jesus our Lord" (Romans 8:38-39 KJV).

Prayer: Lord, thank you that you are praying for us. Amen

Day 214

"His wife Zeresh and all his friends said to him, *'Have a pole set up'*" (Esther 5:14 NIV).

"And I, if I be lifted up from the earth, will draw all men unto me. This he said, signifying what death he should die" (John 12:32-33 KJV).

The pole represents the cross. Jesus was lifted up on the cross for us, for our salvation.

Jesus told Nicodemus: "And as Moses lifted up the serpent in the wilderness, even so must the Son of man be lifted up" (John 3:14 KJV).

When the Israelites were traveling in the desert, they got impatient and complained against God and Moses. They wanted to be back in Egypt (even though they had been slaves there), not die in the desert. They complained that there was no food or water in the wilderness. The Lord grew tired of their complaints and sent poisonous snakes that bit them; many died. The people realized their sin and asked Moses to pray to the Lord to take the snakes away. The Lord told Moses to make a snake and put it on a pole; anyone who would look up to it would live. So Moses made a brass snake; those who looked at it lived. (See Numbers 21:4-9.)

Prayer: Thank you, Father, that we can look to Jesus on the cross and live. Amen

Day 215

"Reaching to a height of fifty cubits, and ask the king in the morning *to have Mordecai impaled on it"* (Esther 5:14 NIV).

"God presented Christ as a sacrifice of atonement, through the shedding of his blood—to be received by faith" (Romans 3:25 NIV).

Fifty represents the year of Jubilee. (See Leviticus 25.) In this fiftieth year the Israelites were to return to their families' property. They were not to plant or harvest; it was to be a holy year to the Lord. The year of Jubilee began on the Day of Atonement. The Day of Atonement was a day an animal was sacrificed and its blood was shed to cover the sins of the people. (See Leviticus 16.)

When Jesus shed his blood on the cross, "God was reconciling the world to himself in Christ, not counting people's sins against them" (2 Corinthians 5:19 NIV). Jesus took the punishment of our sins upon himself on the cross so that we could be reconciled to God.

Prayer: Jesus, thank you for taking the punishment for our sins; your blood washes us clean when we believe in you. Amen

Esther Chapter 5

"Then go with the king to the banquet and enjoy yourself" (Esther 5:14 NIV).

"He brought me to the banqueting house, and his banner over me was love" (Song of Solomon 2:4 KJV).

God's people will come from the east, west, north and south to sit down with Abraham and Isaac and Jacob to enjoy the banquet the Lord has for them. There will be plenty of food and delicious meats and the best wines. There will be no more death, and tears will be wiped away by the Lord himself. The people will say it was good for us to trust the Lord because he has saved us. Now is the time to rejoice in his salvation. (See Matthew 8:11 and Isaiah 25:6-9.)

Prayer: Lord, we look forward to the day when we will sit at the banquet table with you. Amen

Day 217

"This suggestion delighted Haman" (Esther 5:14 NIV).

"And Judas Iscariot, one of the twelve, went unto the chief priests, to betray [Jesus] unto them. And when they heard it, they were glad, and promised to give him money" (Mark 14:10-11 KJV).

The religious rulers of the day were delighted that someone was going to hand Jesus over to them; they were jealous of Jesus' popularity and status among the people. When they had sent the temple guards to arrest Jesus, the guards came back without him. The chief priests and Pharisees asked why hadn't they brought Jesus, they replied that they had never heard anyone speak like him.

The religious leaders claimed that this man Jesus could not be the Messiah, because he was from Galilee and the Holy Scriptures never mentioned a prophet would come from there. (See John 7:45-52.) Actually, Jesus was born in Bethlehem (see Matthew 2:1) and the scripture that prophesied about that is in Micah 5:2.

Prayer: Jesus, you are the Messiah, the promised one of Israel sent to redeem the whole world. May your people, Israel, come to believe in you. Amen

"And he had the pole set up" (Esther 5:14 NIV).

"And [Judas] sought how he might conveniently betray [Jesus]" (Mark 14:11 KJV).

Things were being set up for the betrayal of Jesus by Judas.

The people were divided on how they felt about Jesus. Large crowds followed him and listened to his teachings and were amazed at the authority with which he spoke. Thousands were fed with a few fish and loaves of bread and that was impressive. Many were healed of diseases and sicknesses and demons were cast out. The people asked themselves if this could be the Messiah. People in his hometown wondered where he got his power, because they knew his family, and they were nothing special.

The chief priests and Pharisees feared for their place of authority because Jesus was so popular. Many of the rulers believed in him but would not openly admit it because they feared they would be put out of the synagogue by the Pharisees. "For they loved the praise of men more than the praise of God" (John 12:43 KJV).

Prayer: Lord, may we not love the praise of people more than praise from you. Amen

Day 219

Chapter 5 Review

Day 184: We were made for God.

Day 187: Our wealth in the physical world doesn't gain us favor in the spiritual realm.

Day 192: Each day we have a banquet of choices to feast on. Do we choose "life" or "death"?

Day 196: In prayer, present your requests, not demands; God is in charge.

Day 196: Lord, may we not make vows quickly or take them lightly.

Day 201: If we do today what the Lord says, then tomorrow we will have only tomorrow's assignments to do; not today's and tomorrow's.

Day 202: The Lord wants to be our main source of joy, and the pain reliever for our souls.

Day 212: So, go ahead, take the kingdom of God by storm. Be all in, go all out, be prayed up, and get down to business with God. You only have a limited time here, so give it all you've got.

Prayer: Lord, reveal yourself to us today. Amen

Chapter 5 Challenge

Fill in the blank.

1. _____ days later, Esther approached the king. (5:1)

2. When the king saw the queen, he held out the _____ _____. (5:2)

3. The king asked her what she wanted. He offered her half the _____. (5:3)

4. Esther invited the king and _____ to come to a banquet she had made for them. (5:4-5)

5. _____ left the dinner happy until he saw that _____ didn't rise to show him honor. (5:9)

6. He called his friends together and boasted about his _____, _____ and his high position the king had given him. (5:11)

7. But he couldn't be satisfied until he did something about that man _____. (5:13)

8. His _____ and friends suggested he set up a _____ for the man he despised. (5:14)

Prayer: Lord, keep us from the evil one. Amen

Day 221

"That night the king could not sleep" (Esther 6:1 NIV).
"And [the king] could not sleep" (Daniel 6:18 NIV).

Daniel, an Israelite, was brought to Babylon with others to work for the king there. In time, Daniel had risen to a high place of authority and King Darius planned to promote him over the whole land. Daniel's co-workers were jealous of him and tried to find a way to get him in trouble. They went to the king and asked him to make a law that no one could pray to anyone but the king for thirty days. The king agreed.

When Daniel heard about the new law he prayed to God as usual, with the windows open. The men told the king and Daniel was thrown in with the lions. King Darius liked Daniel and hoped his God, whom he served faithfully, would rescue him. That night he didn't sleep.

The next morning the king went to the den and Daniel was brought out—alive and well. The king then wrote a new law that everyone in his kingdom was to fear the God of Daniel.

Today as God saves us from the lions (see 1 Peter 5:8) our testimony can have a powerful influence on others, just as Daniel's miraculous escape had on King Darius.

Prayer: Lord, give us courage to stay true to you. Amen

Esther Chapter 6

"So he ordered the book of the chronicles, the record of his reign, to be brought in and read to him" (Esther 6:1 NIV).

"The rest of the acts ... and how he reigned, behold, they are written in the book of the chronicles of the kings" (1 Kings 14:19 KJV).

The Bible is the record of God's reign over the earth:

In Genesis 1-2, God created the world and made people in his image.

In Genesis 3, Adam and Eve disobeyed God and sin entered the world.

In Genesis 6-9, God saved Noah and his family from a worldwide flood—God's judgment on sinful humanity.

In Genesis 12 through Malachi, God called Abraham and through his descendants the Lord claimed a people, the Israelites, for himself. They were not faithful to God, so he raised up prophets to tell the Israelites to return to him.

In Matthew through John, God's son was revealed. He was the promised Messiah, the Savior. Jesus came to reconcile the world to God.

In Acts through Revelation, God was at work through his church, drawing Jews and Gentles to himself.

Throughout history God has been calling people to himself. He is still calling today.

Prayer: Thank you, Lord, for the Bible, the record of your reign, that you have kept safe through the centuries. Amen

Day 223

"It was found recorded there that Mordecai had exposed Bigthana and Teresh, two of the king's officers who guarded the doorway, who had conspired to assassinate King Xerxes" (Esther 6:2 NIV).

"Have nothing to do with the fruitless deeds of darkness, but rather expose them" (Ephesians 5:11 NIV).

This is what Mordecai had done; he had exposed the king's officers.

Mordecai who represents Christ, also exposed wrongdoers. Jesus said the Pharisees clean up good on the outside but inside they are wicked. They love occupying the important seats in a gathering and getting respect around town. He warned his disciples about their hypocrisy. He said things that are hidden will become known.

Paul said when the Lord returns that which is hidden in the dark will be brought out into the light and the secrets of the heart will be exposed. (See 1 Corinthians 4:5.)

Prayer: Lord, nothing is hidden from your sight. May we be people of the Light. Amen

Day 224

"'What honor and recognition has Mordecai received for this?' the king asked" (Esther 6:3 NIV).

"Therefore will I divide him a portion with the great ... because he [has] poured out his soul unto death" (Isaiah 53:12 KJV).

Isaiah 53:12, was a prophecy about Jesus. The Jews expected a Messiah that would come in greatness just as the Scriptures foretold. What they didn't understand was that when he came the first time, he wasn't going to establish an earthy kingdom.

One time, Jesus feed over five thousand people with just five loaves of bread and two small fish. Many people were amazed at this and thought he must be the Prophet that they were waiting for. Jesus, knowing their intent to make him king, went away alone to a mountain.

Later on, he was killed. On earth it seemed he died defeated by his enemies, but in heaven there was great rejoicing—this was a victory, not a defeat! A tremendous, marvelous event had just taken place. The Son of God made a way for God to have many sons and daughters! He was raised to life and God has given him the greatest position of all as King of kings and Lord of lords.

Prayer: Lord, we honor and recognize you as King of kings and Lord of lords! Amen

Day 225

"'Nothing has been done for him,' his attendants answered" (Esther 6:3 NIV).

"[Christ] made himself of no reputation, and took upon him the form of a servant, and was made in the likeness of men" (Philippians 2:7 KJV).

In John 13:2-17, Jesus and the disciples were eating a last meal together. Jesus got up. With a towel and a bowl of water he began washing and drying his disciples' feet. (This job was usually done by servants.) Jesus said he was setting an example for them so that they too would wash each other's feet. In other words, they were to humbly serve each other.

His kingdom was not set up in a city with a throne and a palace; he set up his kingdom in the hearts of people. "The kingdom of God is within you" (Luke 17:21 KJV). This foot washing was yet another lesson in kingdom living that Jesus taught them before he left to go to the cross.

Prayer: Lord, may we humbly serve you by serving our brothers and sisters in Christ. Amen

Day 226

"The king said, 'Who is in the court?'" (Esther 6:4 NIV).
"Who will go for us?" (Isaiah 6:8 KJV).

King Xerxes was looking for someone to do a job for him.

God is looking for someone to do a job for him; to be his representative on the earth. "I heard the voice of the Lord, saying, Whom shall I send, and who will go for us? [Isaiah said,] Here am I. Send me" (Isaiah 6:8 KJV).

Isaiah was a prophet called by God to proclaim God's judgment over Israel and all the wicked nations of the world. God also used Isaiah to give hope to the people by prophesying about the coming of the Messiah, the Savior of the world. Here are a few prophesies he gave about the Messiah:

<u>His Birth</u>: "Behold, a virgin shall conceive, and bear a son, and shall call his name Immanuel." "For unto us a child is born, unto us a son is given."

<u>His Ministry</u>: "Be strong, fear not: behold, your God will come ... he will come and save you. Then the eyes of the blind shall be opened, and the ears of the deaf shall be unstopped. Then shall the lame man leap as an hart, and the tongue of the dumb sing."

<u>His Death</u>: "The LORD [has] laid on him the iniquity of us all." "He was cut off out of the land of the living: for the transgression of my people was he stricken."

(Isaiah 7:14, 9:6, 35:4-6, 53:6, 8 KJV).

Prayer: Thank you, God, for coming and saving us. Amen

Day 227

"Now Haman had just entered the outer court of the palace to speak to the king about impaling Mordecai on the pole he had set up for him" (Esther 6:4 NIV).

The chief priests met together to plan how they might kill Jesus. (See Matthew 26:3-4.)

Satan was at work in the religious authorities. The "religious" people of that day were the ones who gave Jesus the most trouble. They knew a lot about God but they needed to let God change their hearts. Jesus told them they were like the people Isaiah prophesied about: "The Lord said, … this people draw near me with their mouth, and with their lips do [honor] me, but have removed their heart far from me" (Isaiah 29:13 KJV).

The enemy still tries to work in "religious" people and Christian organizations—anywhere he can get a foothold to cause division and strife to thwart the work of God if he can. Christians need to be aware of this and be diligent in keeping themselves humbly following Christ with our eyes fixed on him.

Prayer: Lord, let us not be unaware of the enemy's tactics to cause confusion and division in the church and in Christian endeavors. May we pray for peace and unity. Amen

"And the king's servants said unto him, Behold, Haman [stands] in the court. And the king said, Let him come in" (Esther 6:5 KJV).

"And Pharaoh said, Who is the LORD, that I should obey his voice to let Israel go? I know not the LORD, neither will I let Israel go" (Exodus 5:2 KJV).

The Scriptures tell us that God raised up Pharaoh so that the Lord could display his power and all the world would hear about him. (See Romans 9:17.) God can use anyone and anything to fulfill his purposes. God used Pharaoh's stubbornness to show his power; he sent ten plagues. The plague of blood, frogs, gnats, flies, a plague on livestock, boils, hail, locusts, darkness and on the firstborn. (See Exodus 7-12.)

It is interesting that the first plague God sent was the water changed to blood; Jesus' first miracle was turning water into wine (wine is symbolic of blood). The last plague was the death of the firstborn of the Egyptians. The last act of Christ was the death of the firstborn of God. (See Colossians 1: 18.)

Prayer: Lord, you are the mighty God, nothing can stop you from fulfilling your plan. Amen

Day 229

"When Haman entered, the king asked him, '*What should be done for the man the king delights to honor?*'" (Esther 6:6 NIV).

"If any man serve me, him will my Father [honor]" (John 12:26 KJV).

Jesus said that the Father would honor those who serve him. And God will honor those who show honor to him. (See 1 Samuel 2:30.)

One time, Jesus was at a dinner and noticed how some of the guests picked the best places to sit—places of honor. So he told them a parable about a wedding feast where someone took a seat up front, only to have to move to the back when a more important person showed up. How embarrassing! Jesus said that when you go to these gatherings, the wisest thing to do is to sit in the back. Later, you may be asked by the host to move closer to a better seat. Then you will be honored in front of everyone. Whoever promotes himself will be brought down, but the one who is humble shall be lifted up. (See Luke 14:7-11.)

Prayer: Lord, may we not promote ourselves; but may our honor come from you. Amen

"Now Haman thought to himself, 'Who is there that the king would rather honor than me?'" (Esther 6:6 NIV).

"I will be like the most High" (Isaiah 14:14 KJV).

Haman thought very highly of himself. Haman represents Satan. (He is called Lucifer in Isaiah 14:12 KJV.) Satan in his pride was not satisfied with the position God gave him, but wanted to be equal with God. God created him as an angel, a high-ranking angel; but he became proud of his beauty and wanted more power and honor than he was entitled to. (See Isaiah 14:12-15 ; Ezekiel 28:13-17.)

We need to be careful about falling into pride. It is because of our sinful human condition that we want to be looked up to or be admired so that we are above others. Even Jesus' disciples fell prey to this; they argued with each other about which one of them was the greatest disciple. (See Luke 22:24.)

Prayer: Lord, help us not to exalt ourselves above others. Amen

Day 231

In Esther 6:7-11, the horse and rider represent Jesus and his ride into Jerusalem. This event is portrayed in all four of the Gospels.

"And Haman answered the king, For the man whom the king [delights to honor]" (Esther 6:7 KJV).

"When they heard that Jesus was coming to Jerusalem, [they] Took branches of palm trees, and went forth to meet him, and cried, Hosanna: Blessed is the King of Israel that [comes] in the name of the Lord" (John 12:12-13 KJV).

"Have them bring a royal robe the king has worn and a horse the king has ridden, one with a royal crest placed on its head" (Esther 6:8 NIV).

"And Jesus, when he had found a young [donkey, sat on him]; as it is written, Fear not, daughter of Sion: behold [your King comes], sitting on [a donkey's] colt" (John 12:14-15 KJV). Zechariah 9:9 is a prophesy about this event; Zechariah tells the daughters of Zion and Jerusalem to rejoice and shout, for their King is coming with justice and salvation, humbly riding a donkey.

Prayer: Jesus, even in your day of earthly recognition you choose to ride a donkey instead of a fine horse. Help us to follow your example of humility. Amen

"Then let the robe and the horse be entrusted to one of the king's most noble princes" (Esther 6:9 NIV).

Jesus sent two of his disciples into town to find a donkey's colt. (See Mark 11:1-2.) The noble princes represent the disciples.

"Let them robe the man the king delights to honor" (Esther 6:9 NIV).

"And they brought the colt to Jesus, and cast their garments on him; and he sat upon him" (Mark 11:7 KJV). The robe represents the garments.

"And lead him on the horse through the city streets" (Esther 6:9 NIV).

As Jesus was riding the donkey through the city streets, the people cut off branches from the trees and laid them in front of him. Then they shouted aloud. (See Mark 11:8-9.) The horse represents the donkey.

"Proclaiming before him, 'This is what is done for the man the king delights to honor!'" (Esther 6:9 NIV).

They proclaimed: "Hosanna; Blessed is he that [comes] in the name of the Lord" (Mark 11:9 KJV). The king honoring Mordecai represents God honoring Jesus.

Prayer: Blessed be the name of the Lord. Hosanna! Amen

Day 233

"'Go at once,' the king command Haman. *'Get the robe and the horse and do just as you have suggested'"* (Esther 6:10 NIV).

"Go ... into the village ... [and you] shall find a colt tied, [that never has been ridden]: loose him, and bring him" (Luke 19:30 KJV).

"For Mordecai the Jew, who sits at the king's gate" (Esther 6:10 NIV).

"And they brought him to Jesus: and they cast their garments upon the colt, and they set Jesus [on him]" (Luke 19:35 KJV).

"Do not neglect anything you have recommended" (Esther 6:10 NIV).

As they were getting the colt, the owners of the colt asked them why they were taking their animal. The disciples told them they were taking the donkey because the Lord needed him. (See Luke 19:33-34.)

Prayer: Lord, our obedience to you often involves others; please work that out by granting us favor with them. Amen

"So Haman got the robe and the horse. He robed Mordecai" (Esther 6:11 NIV).

"And the disciples went, and did as Jesus commanded them" (Matthew 21:6 KJV). This verse in Matthew 21:6 is a good example for us to follow.

"And led him on horseback through the city streets" (Esther 6:11 NIV).

"And a very great multitude spread their garments in the way; others cut down branches from the trees, and [spread] them in the way" (Matthew 21:8 KJV).

"Proclaiming before him" (Esther 6:11 NIV).

"Hosanna to the Son of David: Blessed is he that [comes] in the name of the Lord; Hosanna in the highest" (Matthew 21:9 KJV).

"This is what is done for the man the king delights to honor!" (Esther 6:11 NIV).

"And when he was come into Jerusalem, all the city was moved, saying, Who is this? And the multitude said, This is Jesus the prophet of Nazareth of Galilee" (Matthew 21:10-11 KJV).

Prayer: Lord, may we honor you by obeying your commands. Amen

Day 235

"Afterward Mordecai returned to the king's gate" (Esther 6:12 NIV).

"Jesus went into the temple of God" (Matthew 21:12 KJV).

Right after Jesus' triumphal entry into Jerusalem he "went into the temple of God, and cast out all them that sold and bought in the temple, and overthrew the tables of the moneychangers, and the seats of them that sold doves, And said unto them, It is written, My house shall be called the house of prayer; but [you] have made it a den of thieves" (Matthew 21:12-13 KJV).

Just as Jesus did a sort of spring cleaning at the temple, sometimes we need a spring cleaning of our temple. "[You] are the temple of the living God" (2 Corinthians 6:16 KJV). In a thorough spring cleaning, some things are washed, other things are given to someone else, and other things are thrown away. We need the Lord to wash us clean in areas where we are dirty. We need to give love, care and compassion to others. We need to toss out unforgiveness, pride and unbelief.

Prayer: Lord, do a spring cleaning in our hearts, we pray. Amen

"But Haman rushed home, with his head covered in grief" (Esther 6:12 NIV).

"Should you then seek great things for yourself? Do not seek them" (Jeremiah 45:5 NIV).

Haman wanted the king to honor him; instead, his enemy Mordecai was honored by the king. This was quite a blow to his ego. Not long before, the king had given his signet ring to Haman (see Esther 3:10) with the freedom and authority to do what he wanted to the Jews.

We shouldn't seek greatness—we should seek God. (Jeremiah 29:13.)

We shouldn't seek revenge—we should seek God. (Romans 12:19.)

We shouldn't seek riches—we should seek God. (1 Timothy 6:9-10.)

We shouldn't seek to please ourselves—we should seek to please God. (John 5:30.)

Prayer: Lord, may we seek you today—and none other. Amen

Day 237

"And [Haman] told Zeresh his wife and all his friends everything that had happened to him" (Esther 6:13 NIV).
"A fool [utters] all his mind" (Proverbs 29:11 KJV).

Hezekiah the king of Judah became ill. The prophet Isaiah was sent to him by the Lord to tell him to put his affairs in order because he was not going to recover from this sickness. Hezekiah wept and pleaded with God for his life and the Lord healed him.

Soon after, representatives of the king of Babylon were sent to Hezekiah because they had heard of his sickness. Hezekiah received them warmly. He showed them his supply of silver and gold and all of his treasures. He told them all about the kingdom and its riches; he withheld nothing.

After they left, Isaiah visited Hezekiah and asked him where those men came from and what they wanted. He told Isaiah they were from far away Babylon. Isaiah asked him what had they seen. Hezekiah told Isaiah that they had seen everything. Isaiah told him the word from the Lord was that in the future all the riches he had shown the men would be carried off to Babylon. (See 2 Kings 20.)

Jesus said not to toss your jewels to pigs; they may trample them and turn back to attack you. (See Matthew 7:6.)

Prayer: Lord, help us to be wise in what we say to others. Amen

"[Haman's] advisers and his wife Zeresh said to him, *'Since Mordecai, before whom your downfall has started, is of Jewish origin'"* (Esther 6:13 NIV).

"There is neither Jew nor Greek, ... for [you] are all one in Christ Jesus" (Galatians 3:28 KJV).

Gentiles were once far away from God; but now they have been brought near because of the blood of Christ. The two groups, Jews and Gentiles, were once divided; but now they are made one by the cross. (See Ephesians 2:11-18.) "For by one Spirit [we are] all baptized into one body, whether we be Jews or Gentiles" (1 Corinthians 12:13 KJV). Those who know Christ as their Savior are no longer Jews or Gentiles, but the body of Christ: the church, his bride. In Christ, we are all in God's family.

This was once a mystery, but it was given to Paul by revelation: In Christ, Gentiles are heirs with Israel, they both are members of one body—the body of Christ. (See Ephesians 3:1-6.)

"For there is no difference between the Jew and the Greek (non-Jew): for the same Lord over all is rich unto all that call upon him. For whosoever shall call upon the name of the Lord shall be saved" (Romans 10:12-13 KJV).

Prayer: Thank you, God, that you love us all and your salvation is for everyone. Amen

Day 239

"You cannot stand against him—you will surely come to ruin!" (Esther 6:13 NIV).

"If it be of God, [you] cannot overthrow it" (Acts 5:39 KJV).

In Acts 5, Peter and the other apostles were working miracles and the religious leaders were jealous. They had the apostles put in prison, but an angel from God came at night and let them out. In the morning, they were preaching about Jesus in the temple and they were arrested again and questioned by the high priests and the Sanhedrin.

A respected Pharisee named Gamaliel, gave the Sanhedrin some wise counsel. He told them to be careful how they treated these men. He then cited other cases where men had gained followers, and they were killed and their followers scattered. He advised the Sanhedrin to let the apostles go, because if their cause was merely a human endeavor, it wouldn't last. But if these men were sent by God, the priests would be at odds with God, and they would surely lose. (See Acts 5:12-39.)

Prayer: God, may we work with you, not against you. It will be for our own good. Amen

"While they were still talking with him, *the king's eunuchs arrived and hurried Haman away* to the banquet Esther had prepared" (Esther 6:14 NIV).

"Resist the devil, and he will flee from you" (James 4:7 KJV).

The king's eunuchs (Holy Spirit) arrived and hurried Haman (Satan) away. When light arrives, darkness flees.

Jesus is the light that came into the world to dispel the darkness. There is darkness in all of us until Jesus comes with his piercing light to penetrate even the hardest heart. Once he arrives, it is his intent to search out each room in our heart and take his light there. Some rooms we may not want him to go in, they are so messy; so we close the door. He won't barge in, but will politely knock. (See Revelation 3:20.) If we don't open that door, he will choose another room. But he will return to that area in our life and knock again and want to enter and have his light illuminate the room with his goodness. He will continue to go from room to room until all our heart is alight with his glory.

Prayer: Lord, help me to allow you access to every room in my heart, so that you can bring the light of your presence there. Amen

Day 241

Day 222: The Bible is the record of God's reign over the earth.

Day 224: On earth it seemed Christ died defeated by his enemies, but in heaven there was great rejoicing—this was a victory not a defeat!

Day 228: God can use anyone and anything to fulfill his purposes.

Day 229: God will honor those who show honor to him.

Day 231: Jesus, even in your day of earthly recognition you chose to ride a donkey instead of a fine horse. Help us to follow your example of humility.

Day 233: Lord, our obedience to you often involves others; please work that out by granting us favor with them.

Day 235: Sometimes we need a spring cleaning of our temple.

Day 236: We shouldn't seek greatness—we should seek God.

Prayer: Lord, may our lives give you honor. Amen

241   Esther Chapter 6

Chapter 6 Challenge

Multiple choice.

1. That very night the king was unable to (eat, sleep or travel). (6:1)

2. He ordered that (Esther, Haman or his record book) be brought to him. (6:1)

3. The king found out that (Haman, Mordecai or Esther) had (plotted, exposed or covered up) an attempt to kill him. (6:2)

4. King Xerxes asked his attendants what (punishment, fine or reward) was given to this person. (6:3)

5. (Nothing, gold or imprisonment) was given, they answered. (6:3)

6. Haman thought the king was going to honor (Esther, Mordecai or himself). (6:6)

7. So, (Mordecai, Esther or Haman) was paraded through town and it was proclaimed that this person was being honored by the king. (6:11)

Prayer: Thank you, God. you are able to arrange things to have your will done. Amen

Day 243

"So the king and Haman went to Queen Esther's banquet" (Esther 7:1 NIV).

"I find then a law, that, when I would do good, evil is present with me" (Romans 7:21 KJV).

Haman (Satan) was right there with Esther (the bride of Christ); the king (God) was also there. God is always with us; we do not face the enemy alone.

Throughout our lives, there will always be the tension of good vs. evil. (Notice the one letter difference between good and God, and evil and devil.) But Christians have Christ to help us fight our battles and make the right choices. God has given the Bible to tell us about him and his ways. We can read about Jesus and see his example of how to live a life pleasing to the Father.

We have the Holy Spirit inside to direct us to the right and to convict us when we do wrong. And (hopefully), we have a church family where we can get love, support and even wise counsel from.

Prayer: Lord, be with us as we face the trials and temptations of life. Guide us to make the right choices. Amen

"And as they were drinking wine on the second day" (Esther 7:2 NIV).

"This is he that came by water and blood, even Jesus Christ" (1 John 5:6 KJV).

The "second day" represents water. On the second day of creation God separated the waters: the water above in the sky from the water below on the earth—the rain from the sea. (See Genesis 1:6-10.) The water above represents the living water, Jesus who came from above. (See John 4:10, 13-14.) The water below represents the natural water. Just as water comes down to the earth and in time evaporates and returns to the sky, so Jesus came down from heaven for a time and then returned to heaven.

The "wine" represents blood. When Jesus was on the cross and the soldiers saw that he was already dead, one of them speared his side and blood and water gushed out. (See John 19:34.) Just as water washes the physical body, Christ "washed us from our sins in his own blood" (Revelation 1:5 KJV).

Prayer: Thank you, Jesus; your blood washes away our sins and your living water gives us life forever. Amen

Day 245

"The king again asked, 'Queen Esther, what is your petition? It will be given you. What is your request?'" (Esther 7:2 NIV).

"For this thing I [sought] the Lord [three times], that it might depart from me" (2 Corinthians 12:8 KJV).

This was the third time the king asked Esther what it was she wanted.

The Apostle Paul had a request: he asked the Lord three times to remove what Paul called a "thorn" sent by Satan. This was something painful in Paul's body or life. The Lord had given him many spiritual revelations, and this thorn was what God was using to keep him from pride. The Lord told him he was not going to deliver him from the distress of the thorn, but give him grace to endure it. "My grace is sufficient for [you]; for my strength is made perfect in weakness" (2 Corinthians 12:9 KJV).

Prayer: Lord, may we rely on your strength each day and not our own. Amen

"Even up to half the kingdom, it will be granted" (Esther 7:2 NIV).

"Whatever you ask I will give you, up to half my kingdom" (Mark 6:23 NIV).

On King Herod's birthday, he gave a banquet for his military leaders and the prominent men of Galilee. When the daughter of his wife Herodias pleased Herod with her dancing he offered her anything she wanted—even half of his kingdom. (See Mark 6:21-23.) Both King Xerxes and King Herod were willing to give away "up to half" of their kingdom.

God doesn't mention a "half" when he promises his kingdom. "For it is your Father's good pleasure to give you the kingdom" (Luke 12:32 KJV). God wants us in his kingdom; that is why he sent his Son, to make a way for us to be included.

Prayer: Father, thank you that Jesus made it possible for us to be a part of your kingdom. Amen

Day 247

"Then Queen Esther answered, *'If I have found favor with you, Your Majesty'*" (Esther 7:3 NIV).

"'Lord,' he said, 'if I have found favor in your eyes'" (Exodus 34:9 NIV).

The Lord promised the Israelites that if they would obey him, they would have his favor. He would do wonders through them that had never been done before and he would drive out their enemies. They were not to make treaties with the other nations. The Israelites were to destroy pagan idols and worship only the Lord because he is a jealous God. He warned them that if they intermarried with the people of the heathen lands, they would surely get involved in idol worship. (See Exodus 34.)

God's will for his people today is the same. He wants to do wonders through his church. (John 14:12) If we obey him, he will drive out our enemies. (Luke 10:19) We are not to compromise our stand with the Lord. (2 Corinthians 6:17) We are to worship the Lord only; he is a jealous God. (1 John 5:21) Christians should not marry unbelievers. (2 Corinthians 6:14)

Prayer: Lord, help us to heed your word and obey your commands. Amen

"And if it pleases you, grant me my life—this is my petition" (Esther 7:3 NIV).

"The gift of God is eternal life" (Romans 6:23 KJV).

We are spiritually dead because of our sins; but God grants us life when we believe in Christ. (See Colossians 2:13.) We ask God for our lives and then in turn we give our lives back to him in service and submission to his will and purposes.

Jesus said, "If any man will come after me, let him deny himself, and take up his cross daily, and follow me. For whosoever will save his life shall lose it: but whosoever will lose his life for my sake, the same shall save it. For what is a man advantaged, if he gain the whole world and lose himself, or be cast away?" (Luke 9:23-25 KJV).

If we live our lives for ourselves we will lose them; but if we live our lives for Christ we will save them. And what in the world is worth more than eternal life with God? Nothing.

Prayer: Lord, may we give away our lives to you because that is the only way to keep them. Amen

Day 249

"And spare my people—this is my request" (Esther 7:3 NIV).

"Spare [your] people, O LORD" (Joel 2:17 KJV).

While Abraham was sitting at the door of his tent, he saw three men approaching. It was the Lord and two of his angels. The Lord promised him a son. (Abraham and Sarah were both too old to have children.) God said, "Is anything too hard for the LORD?" (Genesis 18:14 KJV).

Then the Lord and the two angels headed toward the city of Sodom. The Lord decided to let Abraham in on what was about to happen. Sodom was very wicked and the Lord planned to destroy it.

Abraham asked the Lord if he was going to destroy the righteous people along with the wicked. He asked the Lord to spare the city if there were fifty righteous people; the Lord said he would spare it for the fifty. Abraham asked if he would spare the city for forty-five righteous people; the Lord said he would spare it for forty-five. Abraham kept asking a smaller number until he got down to ten. The Lord said he would spare it for ten righteous people.

But the Lord didn't find even ten righteous people, and he had the city destroyed; but only after the angels got Abraham's nephew Lot and his family out. (See Genesis 18-19.)

Prayer: Spare your righteous people, Lord. Amen

"For I and my people have been sold to be destroyed, killed and annihilated" (Esther 7:4 NIV).

"And the LORD sold them into the hand of Jabin king of Canaan" (Judges 4:2 KJV).

The Israelites had again fallen into evil practices, so the Lord was punishing them by allowing their enemies to pursue them. Sisera was the commander of Jabin's army. He had harassed Israel for twenty years; so the people of Israel called out to the Lord for deliverance.

The prophetess Deborah was a judge and leader of Israel at this time. She had a message from the Lord for Barak, the commander of Israel's army: he was to attack Sisera and the Lord would give Israel the victory. Barak said they would go, but only if Deborah went with them. Deborah told him that because he had to have her along Barak wouldn't get credit for the victory, but a woman.

So the Israelites went out and attacked Sisera and his army. The battle was fierce. Sisera escaped on foot and hid in a tent and fell into an exhausted sleep. The woman whose tent it was killed him while he slept. The word of the Lord came true. Israel defeated their enemies and the honor of killing Sisera went to a woman. (But to his credit Barak is listed in faith's "hall of fame" in Hebrews 11:32.)

Prayer: Lord, you are faithful and true. May we be faithful to you and may you give us victory over our enemies. Amen

Day 251

"If we had merely been *sold as male and female slaves*" (Esther 7:4 NIV).

"I am unspiritual, sold as a slave to sin" (Romans 7:14 NIV).

We are slaves to sin until the Lord sets us free. Even after we believe in Christ there is still a battle to be fought against sin. We can be victorious if we allow the Holy Spirit to fight the battle with us. Continuing to pray for God's help and standing on the word of God give us strength in the battle.

We are enslaved by what we yield to: the consequence of sin is death and the benefit of obedience is life and holy living. (See Romans 6:16.) When we repeatedly sin in an area, we become a slave to it and need the Lord to deliver us. Then we must be diligent to keep that deliverance so the enemy won't trip us up again. (See Galatians 5:1.)

Prayer: Lord, set us free from sin and keep us free by your power. Amen

"I would have kept quiet, because no such distress would justify disturbing the king" (Esther 7:4 NIV).

"You may ask me for anything" (John 14:14 NIV).

How many of us have not prayed about something because it was so small, we felt it wasn't worth disturbing our King? He has so many people and issues to deal with. He has enough big problems to deal with. Why would he want to be bothered with our little problems?

One reason to take anything to the Lord is because he loves us and cares about us personally. He does want to be involved in every area of our lives and every decision we make.

Another reason to pray about little problems is that little problems don't often go away, but grow into bigger problems. If we take our issues to the Lord and ask his help and guidance now, that may save us from a lot of trouble and pain in the future. Also, it pleases him when we follow his directions on how to handle our problems.

Prayer: Lord, thank you that nothing is too small to pray about. Amen

Day 253

"King Xerxes asked Queen Esther, '*Who is he? Where is he—the man who has dared to do such a thing?*'" (Esther 7:5 NIV).

"Lord, who is it?" (John 13:25 KJV).

Jesus was with his disciples and he told them that one of them was going to betray him. They looked at each other, confused by what he had just said. Peter signaled to John to have him ask who would dare do such a thing; so John asked Jesus. Jesus said it was the one whom he would give a piece of bread; and he gave it to Judas. After Judas ate the bread, Satan went into him. Later that night Judas led the soldiers to Jesus and he was arrested. (See John 13:21-27, 18:3) The disciples who were with him ran away.

Haman and Judas were both inspired by Satan and dared to do an evil thing.

Prayer: Lord, keep us safe from the schemes of wicked people. Amen

Day 254

"And Esther said, *'The adversary and enemy is this wicked Haman'"* (Esther 7:6 KJV).

"Your enemy the devil prowls around like a roaring lion looking for someone to devour" (1 Peter 5:8 NIV). KJV says "Your adversary the devil" (1 Peter 5:8).

"Then Haman was afraid before the king" (Esther 7:6 KJV).

"The devils also believe, [in God] and tremble" (James 2:19 KJV).

The demons believe, but do not live for God or follow his ways; they tremble because they know that judgment awaits them. This is a warning to us that just believing in God is not enough; we must act on what we believe.

"And the queen" (Esther 7:6 KJV).

"And these signs shall follow them that believe; In my name they shall cast out devils" (Mark 16:17 KJV). "The seventy [disciples] returned again with joy, saying, Lord, even the devils are subject unto us through [your] name'" (Luke 10:17 KJV).

Jesus has given his church, his bride, authority over the enemy—Satan and his demons are afraid of the power of Jesus.

Prayer: In you, Lord, there is power over the enemy. Amen

Day 255

"The king got up in a rage" (Esther 7:7 NIV).

"The anger of the LORD was hot against Israel" (Judges 2:20 KJV).

The Lord told the Israelites not to worship the idols of Egypt; but they rebelled against him and wouldn't listen and he was angry with them. God planned to release his fury on them in Egypt, but for his name's sake he didn't. Instead he decided to bring them out of Egypt and give them his laws in the wilderness. Yet they still rebelled against him in the wilderness and he planned to destroy them. But for the sake of his good name among the other nations he spared them. Still they continued to reject his commands. (See Ezekiel 20.)

Are our hearts totally devoted to the Lord, or are we serving him and keeping our other gods? Something that we treasure more than the Lord becomes our idol or our god. (See Psalm 24:4; Ezekiel 20:16.) "They feared the LORD, and served their own gods" (2 Kings 17:33 KJV).

Prayer: Lord, deliver us from idols and false gods. Amen

"[The king] left his wine and went out into the palace garden" (Esther 7:7 NIV).

On the cross, "Jesus cried with a loud voice, saying … My God, my God, why [have you] forsaken me?" (Matthew 27:46 KJV).

The wine represents Christ. God temporarily left Jesus. God is a holy God and Jesus at that time was representing sinful humanity. "For [God has] made him to be sin for us, who knew no sin; that we might be made the righteousness of God in him" (2 Corinthians 5:21 KJV).

God turned his back on his Son for a moment because he could not associate with the sins of the human race—his holiness would not permit it. Christ was able to take our place and be a substitution for us; the Father accepted this as payment for the sins of the whole world.

Prayer: Thank you, God, for allowing Jesus to take our punishment for sin. Thank you, Jesus, for willingly being a sacrifice for us. Amen

Day 257

"But Haman, realizing that the king had already decided his fate" (Esther 7:7 NIV).

"The prince of this world [Satan] is judged" (John 16:11 KJV).

God has already decided the devil's future fate: "And the devil ... was cast into the lake of fire and brimstone, ... and shall be tormented day and night for ever and ever" (Revelation 20:10 KJV).

Also, God didn't spare the angels that sinned by leaving their proper place, but chained them in the darkness of hell until the judgment day. (See 2 Peter 2:4; Jude 1:6.)

"Stayed behind to beg Queen Esther for his life" (Esther 7:7 NIV).

The demons in the demon-possessed men begged Jesus to let them go into the herd of pigs. Jesus did as they asked; the herd went running into the sea and died. (See Matthew 8:28-32.)

Prayer: Thank you, Lord, that you will deal with the devil and the fallen angels. Amen

Esther Chapter 7

"Just as *the king returned* from the palace garden to the banquet hall" (Esther 7:8 NIV).

God returned to Jesus on the cross, and Jesus prayed "Father, into [your] hands I commend my spirit" (Luke 23:46 KJV). Then he bowed his head and died.

"'Return to me, and I will return to you,' says the Lord Almighty" (Malachi 3:7 NIV). God was speaking to the Israelites—they had turned away from him and not kept his commands. Over and over again the Lord called to them to follow him in obedience; they did for a time and then they strayed again. God promised them blessing after blessing if they would obey his voice.

God is speaking today—return to me. Jesus said in the last days because of the evil in the world many will fall away from the faith. (See Matthew 24:10, 12.)

Prayer: Lord, may those who have left return to you, and may you return to them. Amen

Day 259

"Haman was falling" (Esther 7:8 NIV).

"How [you have] fallen from heaven, O Lucifer, son of the morning!" (Isaiah 14:12 KJV).

Jesus said, "I beheld Satan as lightning fall from heaven" (Luke 10:18 KJV). This event is also recorded in Revelation 12:7-9: "And there was war in heaven: Michael and his angels fought against the dragon; and the dragon fought and his angels" (v. 7 KJV). The dragon (Lucifer or Satan) and the angels who sided with him (the fallen angels or demons) lost the battle and were thrown out of heaven and cast to the earth. (This fall of Satan happened before Adam and Eve because he was the tempter—the snake—in the Garden in Genesis 3.)

Prayer: Father, keep us from falling for the lies of the devil. Amen

"On the couch where Esther was reclining" (Esther 7:8 NIV).

"Why are you sleeping? ... Get up and pray" (Luke 22:46 NIV).

Haman is headed toward Esther and she is reclining on the couch.

The devil is attacking the church. Will we take this lying down?

On the most difficult night in Jesus' life he asked his disciples to pray. For him? No, for themselves, that they not yield to temptation. Jesus then went away to pray and he was deeply distressed. After praying he returned to his disciples and found them sleeping. He asked them,

"Couldn't you keep watch for one hour? Watch and pray so that you will not fall into temptation. The spirit is willing, but the flesh is weak" (Mark 14:37-38 NIV).

Are we willing to get up off the couch or bed and pray? Pray for God to work in our family, friends, world and us. Pray for a move of the Spirit in our lives and in the church so we will be a force for good in this world of evil.

Prayer: Lord, help us to pray. Amen

Day 261

"The king exclaimed, 'Will *he even molest the queen* while she is with me in the house?'" (Esther 7:8 NIV).

"For the accuser of our brethren [Satan] is cast down, which accused them before our God day and night" (Revelation 12:10 KJV).

Satan molests the church, the bride, but only for a season; God allows this for the purpose of purifying, so that she will become like Christ.

"We are troubled on every side, yet not distressed; we are perplexed, but not in despair; Persecuted, but not forsaken; cast down, but not destroyed; Always bearing about in the body the dying of the Lord Jesus, that the life also of Jesus might be made manifest in our body" (2 Corinthians 4:8-10 KJV).

"Who shall separate us from the love of Christ? shall tribulation, or distress, or persecution, or famine, or nakedness, or peril, or sword? ... [No], in all these things we are more than conquerors through him that loved us" (Romans 8:35, 37 KJV).

God is greater than anything we may face in this world.

Prayer: Lord, help us in our trials to look to you for help and guidance. Amen

"As soon as the word left the king's mouth, they covered Haman's face" (Esther 7:8 NIV).

"None of my words [will] be prolonged any more, but the word which I have spoken shall be done, [says] the LORD GOD" (Ezekiel 12:28 KJV).

Here are some verses about the word of the Lord:

"The word of the LORD is right" (Psalm 33:4 KJV).

"[Your] word have I hid in [my] heart, that I might not sin" (Psalm 119:11 KJV).

"[Your] word is a lamp unto my feet, and a light unto my path" (Psalm 119:105 KJV).

"[Your] word is true from the beginning" (Psalm 119:160 KJV).

"The word is near you; it is in your mouth and in your heart" (Romans 10:8 NIV).

"The word of God is ... a discerner of the thoughts and intents of the heart" (Hebrews 4:12 KJV).

Prayer: May we live by your word, Lord. Amen

Day 263

"Then Harbona, one of the eunuchs attending the king, said, 'A *pole* reaching to a height of fifty cubits stands by Haman's house'" (Esther 7:9 NIV).

Jesus became "obedient unto death, even the death of the cross" (Philippians 2:8 KJV).

Haman had a pole set up for Mordecai, as Satan had a cross set up for Christ.

It was God's predetermined plan that Jesus would go to the cross. Afterward God raised him up; death could not hold him. (See Acts 2:23-24.)

"He had it set up for Mordecai, who spoke up to help the king" (Esther 7:9 NIV).

"You, with the help of wicked men, put him to death by nailing him to the cross" (Acts 2:23 NIV).

Judas, being influenced by the devil, "set up" Jesus to be arrested.

We may sometimes feel "set-up" by the enemy, but if we are following God, he will not allow the enemy to do anything more than God permits. God is sovereign—his power and authority are unequalled to any other. He reigns supreme.

Prayer: God, thank you that nothing can touch your people except what you allow. Amen

"The king said, 'Impale him on it!'" (Esther 7:9 NIV).
"'Crucify him!' they shouted" (Mark 15:13 NIV).

After Jesus was arrested, he was taken to the high priest and the other religious authorities who had gathered there. There were witnesses there to tell of his wrongdoing, but they gave such conflicting accounts that their testimony didn't amount to much. Jesus remained silent and didn't try to defend himself. When the authorities asked him if he was the Messiah, he replied, "I am." They then accused him of blasphemy and sentenced him to death.

The next morning, they took him to Pilate, the governor, so he could hear their case against Jesus. Later he was taken to Herod; then sent back to Pilate. Pilate said that he could not find a reason for Jesus to be killed; so he planned to punish him and let him go. But the crowd continued to shout that he be crucified. Pilate gave in to their demands and had Jesus crucified. (See Matthew 26-27; Mark 14-15; Luke 22-23; John 18-19.)

Prayer: Jesus, thank you for enduring such ridicule and suffering for us. Amen

Day 265

"So they impaled Haman on the pole he had set up for Mordecai" (Esther 7:10 NIV).

"And having disarmed the powers and authorities, he made a public spectacle of them, triumphing over them by the cross" (Colossians 2:15 NIV).

This represents Satan's defeat; he thought he had destroyed Christ on the cross but the cross only defeated Satan instead. Christ came for this purpose "that he might destroy the works of the devil" (1 John 3:8 KJV).

To Jesus' disciples this looked like the end. Their glorious leader, healer and friend had been crucified. The one they thought was the prophesied Messiah and Savior of the world was now dead. They couldn't believe it. Now what were they going to do? They had left everything to follow him.

But this was not the end. Christ arose victorious over sin, death and the devil. Those who put their trust in Christ can have the same victory!

Prayer: Thank you Lord. You defeated the enemy; he didn't defeat you! Amen

Esther Chapter 7

Day 266

"Then the king's fury subsided" (Esther 7:10 NIV).

"Being now justified by his blood, we shall be saved from wrath through him" (Romans 5:9 KJV).

We who believe, have been saved from God's fury by the sacrifice of his Son. Christ took God's anger against sin upon himself on the cross; those who are in Christ are saved from God's wrath.

There will be a day in the future, at the end of this age, when God's wrath will be poured out on those who have rejected him—they will not be able to buy their way out of it.

Here is a reference to that day in Zephaniah 1:14-18 (KJV): "The great day of the LORD is near …. That day is a day of wrath, a day of trouble and distress … A day of the trumpet and alarm …. And I will bring distress upon men … because they have sinned against the LORD …. Neither their silver nor their gold shall be able to deliver them in the day of the LORD'S wrath."

Prayer: Lord, draw many to you so they won't experience your wrath. Amen

Day 267

Chapter 7 Review

Day 243: God is always with us; we do not face the enemy alone.

Day 248: What in the world is worth more than eternal life with God? Nothing.

Day 251: We are slaves to sin until the Lord sets us free.

Day 254: This is a warning to us that just believing in God is not enough; we must act on what we believe.

Day 255: Something that we treasure more than the Lord becomes our idol or our god.

Day 258: God is speaking today—return to me.

Day 261: Satan molests the church, the bride, but only for a season; God allows this for the purpose of purifying, so that she will become like Christ.

Day 263: We may sometimes feel "set-up" by the enemy, but if we are following God, he will not allow the enemy to do anything more than God permits.

Prayer: Lord, you are greater than any problems we face. Amen

Chapter 7 Challenge

Answer the questions below.

1. At the banquet the king wanted to know Esther's request. What was her request? (7:3)

2. Who was her enemy and the enemy of her people? (7:6)

3. What was the king's response? (7:7)

4. Who begged Esther for his life? (7:7)

5. What did the king accuse Haman of doing? (7:8)

6. What did Harbona tell the king about Haman? (7:9)

7. What happened to Haman? (7:10)

Prayer: Lord, may we trust you to carry us through this life with its perils. Amen

Day 269

"That same day King Xerxes gave Queen Esther the estate of Haman, the enemy of the Jews" (Esther 8:1 NIV).

"Blessed are the meek: for they shall inherit the earth" (Matthew 5:5 KJV).

The king (God) gave Queen Esther (bride of Christ) the land once owned by Haman (Satan). The devil now holds the position of prince of this world. (See John 12:31, 14:30, 16:11.) But one day he will be dethroned and the bride of Christ will take her rightful place. "The righteous shall inherit the land, and dwell [there forever]" (Psalm 37:29 KJV). We are waiting for that promise to be fulfilled.

The Lord wanted the Israelites to inhabit the land he had promised to their forefather Abraham, but they were afraid. (See Numbers 13-14.)

The Lord wants to take us to the land he has promised us. We will need to trust him, not complain and slink back in fear as the Israelites did. Our enemies look strong, but God is stronger. "He that [overcomes] shall inherit all things; and I will be his God, and he shall be my son. But the fearful, and unbelieving ... shall have their part in the lake which [burns] with fire ... which is the second death" (Revelation 21:7-8 KJV).

Prayer: Lord, help us to proceed in faith so that we may inherit what you have promised. Amen

Esther Chapter 8

"And Mordecai came into the presence of the king" (Esther 8:1 NIV).

"I ascend unto my Father" (John 20:17 KJV).

After his resurrection, Christ went into the presence of God for us. He ascended to heaven to offer his blood in the sanctuary, not year after year like the high priest offered blood, but once, a sacrifice for the sins of all people. (See Hebrews 9:22-26.) Now he sits at the right hand of the Father, praying for us.

I've thought about this concept of Jesus praying for us and wondered; if Jesus is praying for us, then why is the world so bad off? It's because we have free will to choose right or wrong. The Lord has given us his Word with directions on how to live. Even those who haven't had any church or Bible background have the laws of the land.

The Israelites had God's laws, but most failed miserably in following him—they got caught up in worshiping the gods of the other nations. And keeping laws doesn't change our wicked hearts, just our outward behavior. Christ came because we needed the power of God to change our hearts, so we could live in harmony with God and with each other.

Prayer: Lord, change our hearts so that we can love and follow you. Amen

Day 271

"For Esther had told how [Mordecai] was related to her" (Esther 8:1 NIV).

"Whoever does God's will is my brother and sister and mother" (Mark 3:35 NIV).

Jesus said that everyone who does the will of God is his relative; they are a brother or sister or mother. Notice it does not mention "father" because he has only one father, the heavenly Father.

Brother:

There were two brothers: their father had told them to go and work in his vineyard. One brother said he wouldn't go, but later he did go and work. The other brother said he would go, but didn't. Which one did the will of the father? The first brother. (See Matthew 21:28-31.)

Sister:

There were two sisters: one was busy preparing the meal for Jesus and his disciples. The other was sitting at Jesus' feet listening to him. Which one did the will of the Father? The second sister. (See Luke 10:38-42.)

Mother:

There were two mothers: one was called to raise the prophet who would proclaim to the world that the Messiah had come. The other was called to raise the Son of God, the Savior of the world. Which did the will of the Father? Both mothers. (See Luke 1.)

Prayer: Thank you, Jesus, that doing the Father's will makes us family. Amen

Esther Chapter 8

"And the king took off his ring, which he had taken from Haman, and gave it unto Mordecai" (Esther 8:2 KJV).

"I [Jesus Christ] am alive ... and have the keys of hell and of death" (Revelation 1:18 KJV).

Christ rescued us from the power of darkness (Satan). The authority and power Satan had over us has been "reclaimed" and given to Christ.

Jesus has power and authority:

"The Son of man [has] power on earth to forgive sins" (Matthew 9:6 KJV).

"All power is given unto [Jesus] in heaven and in earth" (Matthew 28:18 KJV).

"With authority and power he [commands] the unclean spirits, and they come out" (Luke 4:36 KJV).

"The power of the Lord was present to heal them" (Luke 5:17 KJV).

The Father has "given him authority to execute judgment" (John 5:27 KJV).

Prayer: Lord, you are all powerful; nothing is too hard for you. Amen

Day 273

"And Esther set Mordecai over the house of Haman" (Esther 8:2 KJV).

"For the Lord Almighty will reign on Mount Zion and in Jerusalem, and before its elders—with great glory" (Isaiah 24:23 NIV).

In the new earth, under the Lord's reign, he will joyfully lead his people. There will not be sorrow and crying. Children will not die in infancy. God's people will live long lives—a hundred years old will seem young. When they have a house built, they will live there and not have to be concerned about fire or flood destroying it. They will plant gardens and vineyards and eat of the produce because pest or disease will not destroy their crops. The righteous will live long as the trees and enjoy their work for a long time. They and their children will be blessed by the Lord.

"And it shall come to pass, that before they call, I [the Lord] will answer; and while they are yet speaking, I will hear" (Isaiah 65:24).

The wolf and the lamb will eat side by side and the lion will not seek its prey—but eat straw. Nothing will hurt or destroy his people on God's holy mountain—the Lord declares. (See Isaiah 65:17-25.)

Prayer: Lord, we are looking forward to the new earth where you will reign in righteousness. Amen

Esther Chapter 8

Day 274

"Esther again pleaded with the king, falling at his feet and weeping. She begged him to put an end to the evil plan of Haman the Agagite, which he had devised against the Jews" (Esther 8:3 NIV).

Jesus Christ came "that he might deliver us from this present evil world" (Galatians 1:4 KJV).

People throughout the centuries have been pleading with God; falling on their knees and weeping, begging God to put an end to the evil plans of Satan which he has devised against Jews and Christians and everyone else in the world.

There is trouble in every nation, tribe and race; Satan has a foothold all over the earth.

But God is at work, too. He hears the prayers of his people and answers in his time.

In Revelation 6:10-11, the martyrs call out to the Lord, asking how long will it be before he judges the people on the earth and avenge their blood. He tells them they must wait a little longer until the other martyrs arrive.

We also plead for the Lord to come and put an end to the evil in the world.

Prayer: "Come, Lord Jesus" (Revelation 22:20 KJV). Amen

Day 275

"Then the king held out the golden scepter toward Esther" (Esther 8:4 KJV).

"But now in Christ Jesus you who once were far away have been brought near by the blood of Christ" (Ephesians 2:13 NIV).

The king (God) extended the golden scepter (Christ) to Esther (bride of Christ).

God in his mercy has extended Christ to us. That is good news because we need a Savior. Until we find him, we are lost.

If you have ever been traveling and have gotten lost you know that is not a good feeling, especially if you have a certain time you need to be somewhere. The problem (spiritually) with some people is that they don't feel they are lost, so they don't think they need to ask for directions (to find God). They are traveling down the road of life in the direction they feel is right for them, and they don't need your help, "thank you very much." What they don't realize is that the road they are taking leads to death. They will not be pleased when they arrive at their destination.

God has provided the way (Jesus) with directions (the Bible) so that we can reach our destination (heaven) safely and on time.

Prayer: Lord, may we travel through this life with you and into the next. Amen

Day 276

"So Esther arose, and stood before the king" (Esther 8:4 KJV).

"And having done all ... stand" (Ephesians 6:13 KJV).

The Israelites fled from Egypt where they were slaves. Now the Egyptian army was after them. The sea was before them and the army behind. Moses told the people not to be afraid but to stand still and see how the Lord would deliver them. The Lord parted the Red Sea and the Israelites walked through on dry ground and escaped from their enemies. When the Egyptian army tried to do the same, the Lord made the sea come back together and the Egyptians were drowned. (See Exodus 14.)

Esther obeyed Mordecai's instruction (see Esther 4:8), she went to the king to plead for help for her people; then she stood to see what his response would be. We are to obey the Lord's commands, lift our situations to him in prayer, then stand on his promises and wait to see what he will do. After having prayed and obeyed—stand.

Prayer: Lord, let us stand in faith after we pray and expect an answer. Amen

Day 277

"'If it pleases the king' she said, 'and if he regards me with favor and thinks it the right thing to do, and if he is pleased with me'" (Esther 8:5 NIV).

"If it is the Lord's will" (James 4:15 NIV).

James 4:15 is a good verse to incorporate into our prayers. The purpose of prayer is to get to know God and to praise and worship him. Also, to discern his will in any given situation, and to tell him our needs and requests. As we pray for the different people and situations in our lives, let's pray that the Lord's will be done. This helps us to keep a humble attitude and reminds us that it is his will that is important, not ours. He knows what's best.

Prayer: God, may your will be done in the circumstances we lift up to you in prayer. Amen

Esther Chapter 8

"Let an order be written overruling the dispatches that Haman son of Hammedatha, the Agagite, devised and wrote to destroy the Jews in all the king's provinces" (Esther 8:5 NIV).

"For the wages of sin is death; but the gift of God is eternal life through Jesus Christ our Lord" (Romans 6:23 KJV).

Haman's edict was a death sentence to the Jews. Fallen humanity was under a death sentence until Christ came to our rescue. In Christ we have life:

L- Life	"You give life to everything."
I-Immortality	"This mortal [body] must put on immortality."
F- Forever	"And so shall we ever be with the Lord."
E- Eternal	"The gift of God is eternal life through Jesus Christ."

(Nehemiah 9:6 NIV; 1 Corinthians 15:53 KJV; 1 Thessalonians 4:17 KJV; Romans 6:23 KJV)

Prayer: Lord, may we choose life in Christ and live with you eternally. Amen

Day 279

"For how can I bear to see disaster fall on my people? How can I bear to see the destruction of my family?" (Esther 8:6 NIV).

"Whose end is destruction" (Philippians 3:19 KJV).

We and our families are doomed to destruction unless we call on God to save us. Let's continue to pray and seek him on behalf of our families. Pray that he would put godly people in our loved ones' paths to speak to them. We can pray that the Lord would soften their hearts toward the message of the gospel. Also, that he would bring the word of God to their remembrance, for those who were raised hearing about Jesus. And for those who don't have a Bible background; pray the Lord would have them exposed to his Word and the message of the gospel in some way. Ask God that they would see their need of him now and see their need to prepare for eternity.

Prayer: Lord, we pray that you would save our families. Amen

Day 280

"King Xerxes replied to Queen Esther and to Mordecai the Jew, *'Because Haman attacked the Jews'*"(Esther 8:7 NIV).

"People who are wicked and deceitful ... attack me without cause" (Psalm 109:2-3 NIV).

In Genesis 37, begins the story of Joseph, the teenage son of Jacob. Jacob had many sons but Joseph was his favorite. The other sons knew this and hated Joseph; they planned to kill him. When some traders came by; they sold him instead. Joseph ended up in Egypt as a slave to Potiphar, but the Lord was with him. Then Potiphar's wife accused Joseph of trying to rape her and he was thrown in prison. He stayed in prison for years and then was brought out to interpret a dream for Pharaoh. After interpreting Pharaoh's dream, he was promoted.

When there was a famine, Joseph's brothers came to buy food in Egypt and Joseph was the one who sold it to them. He told his brothers, "It was not you that sent me [here], but God." "[You] thought evil against me; but God meant it [for] good" (Genesis 45:8, 50:20 KJV).

Prayer: Lord, when we are treated unjustly, you can use even that for our good and the good of others. Amen

"I have given his estate to Esther, and they impaled him on the pole he set up" (Esther 8:7 NIV).

"Good master, what shall I do that I may inherit eternal life?" (Mark 10:17 KJV).

Esther inherited Haman's estate. How do we inherit eternal life? Here's a story of a rich man who came to Jesus asking that very question.

A man came running to Jesus and fell at his feet. He asked, "Good master, what shall I do that I may inherit eternal life?" Jesus asked him why he called him good; only God is good. He told the man some of the Ten Commandments— don't kill, steal, or commit adultery; don't be a false witness; honor your parents. The man claimed he did all these things his whole life. Jesus loved the man; but knowing the man's heart, Jesus knew he was missing something. Jesus told him to sell all his possessions and give the money to the poor and in heaven he would have treasure. Then, follow him (Jesus). The man went away sadly because he was very rich. Jesus told his disciples that it was hard for rich people to enter the kingdom of God. (See Mark 10:17-23.)

Prayer: Lord, help us not to let riches or anything keep us from your kingdom. Amen

"Now write another decree *in the king's name* in behalf of the Jews as seems best to you" (Esther 8:8 NIV).

"What is his name?" (Exodus 3:13 KJV).

Moses was taking care of his father-in-law's flock when an angel appeared to him in a burning bush. God called to him from the bush and told him to remove his sandals, because he was on holy ground. God introduced himself as the God of his forefathers—Abraham, Isaac and Jacob. Moses turned his head because he was afraid to look at God. God told him he had heard the cries of his people, the Israelites, in Egypt, and he was going to deliver them from their slavery. The Lord said he was going to send Moses to bring them out of Egypt. Moses told God that if he went to rescue the Israelites, they might ask who sent him, and "What is his name?" God answered him saying, "I AM WHO I AM" (Exodus 3:14 NIV).

God's name is "I AM."

I am your provider. I am your salvation. I am your deliverer. I am your healer. I am your Father. I am your everything.

Prayer: Lord God, you are all we need. Amen

Day 283

"And seal it with the king's signet ring" (Esther 8:8 NIV).

"He anointed us, set his seal of ownership on us, and put his Spirit in our hearts as a deposit" (2 Corinthians 1:21-22 NIV).

<u>Anointed</u>. The Lord will save his anointed ones (those who are devoted to him and his purposes). From heaven he hears our prayers and answers them—he saves us with his mighty right hand. Some trust in their own abilities, but we trust in the Lord. Their strength will fail them, but God is our strength and he never fails. (See Psalm 20:6-8.)

<u>Seal of ownership</u>. We have been bought by the precious blood of Christ and now God owns us. No longer are we to live our lives as we please, but to live our lives to please God. We are to live lives that bring honor to God.

<u>His Spirit</u>. For believers, our body is the house of the Holy Spirit. It's his Holy Spirit in us that enables us to live godly lives as we follow his leading. (See 1 Corinthians 6:19-20.)

Prayer: You have sealed us as yours; thank you, Father. Amen

"For no document written in the king's name and sealed with his ring can be revoked" (Esther 8:8 NIV).

"God's solid foundation stands firm, [and] sealed" (2 Timothy 2:19 NIV).

The Bible is a document written by men who were inspired by God. It cannot be revoked: "the word of our God shall stand for ever" (Isaiah 40:8 KJV). Even Jesus said he came to fulfill, not destroy the law and the prophets of the Old Testament. (See Matthew 5:17.)

Jesus said, "Heaven and earth shall pass away, but my words shall not pass away" (Matthew 24:35 KJV). God's word is a firm foundation to stand on. It is eternal truth. Contrary to what some believe, it is not outdated, old-fashioned or irrelevant for today. It has the principles we need to base our lives on.

Jesus said if we hear his words and obey them it's like building a house on a rock. When the winds and floods come, the house will stand and not fall. But if we hear his words and don't obey them, it's like building on sand: when the winds and floods come, the house will fall. (See Matthew 7:24-27.)

Prayer: Lord, may our lives be built on the Rock—you. Amen

Day 285

"At once the royal secretaries were summoned—on the twenty-third day of the third month, the month of Sivan" (Esther 8:9 NIV).

"For he will command his angels" (Psalm 91:11 NIV).

The royal secretaries represent the angels of God.

Here are two stories of angels sent to help the believers:

In Acts 5, the apostles, by the power of the Spirit, were performing miracles and healing the sick. Many people were coming to believe in Jesus through the apostles' preaching and by observing all the miraculous things that were happening. The high priest and the spiritual leaders were jealous of the apostles and had them arrested and put in jail. But God sent an angel during the night and he let them out. The angel told them to keep preaching about Jesus.

In Acts 8:26-38, an angel of the Lord told Philip to go south to a certain road. Then the Spirit told him to meet up with a man coming down the road in a chariot. He met the man, who was reading from the Scriptures as he rode. Philip shared Jesus with him, using the very scriptures the man was reading in the Book of Isaiah. The man believed and was baptized that very day. Then the Holy Spirit took Philip away and he was found at Azotus. He traveled around to the different towns, preaching the gospel wherever he went.

Prayer: Thank you, Lord; you send your angels to help us. Amen

Day 286

"They wrote out all Mordecai's orders to the Jews, and to the satraps, governors and nobles of the 127 provinces stretching from India to Cush" (Esther 8:9 NIV).

"What I am writing to you is the Lord's command" (1 Corinthians 14:37 NIV).

Jesus' command is that we should love God and love our neighbor.

Jesus told this story to tell us what he meant by loving our neighbor:

A man was walking to Jericho when he was robbed, beaten and left to die. A priest coming along the same road saw the man and went on. Another holy man walked by and kept on going. Then another man, a Samaritan, came by and he stopped. He cleaned up and bandaged the man as best he could, then put him on his own donkey and took him to an inn. Once there, he was better able to care for him. The next day the good Samaritan needed to leave. He gave the innkeeper some money and asked him to check on the wounded man later to see if he needed anything.

The person who shows mercy and compassion to someone is loving his/her neighbor. (See Luke 10:29-37.)

Prayer: Lord, help us to show compassion to others. Amen

Day 287

"These orders were written in the script of each province and the language of each people and also to the Jews in their own script and language" (Esther 8:9 NIV).

"With your blood you [Christ] purchased for God persons from every tribe and language and people and nation" (Revelation 5:9 NIV).

The Lord shall have people in his kingdom from every nation and language.

"And there was given him dominion, and glory, and a kingdom, that all people, nations, and languages, should serve him: his dominion is an everlasting dominion, which shall not pass away, and his kingdom ... shall not be destroyed" (Daniel 7:14 KJV).

We don't know if we will all speak the same language in the coming age—the language of heaven, perhaps; or if we will keep our native language, but understand and be able to communicate in all languages. It is a mystery. Things will be so different then—new, God calls it. (See Revelation 21:5.)

We do know it will be good because God is good. What we need to do is follow him faithfully in this life, so that we will be counted worthy to enjoy the next life, eternally with him. (See Luke 21:36.)

Prayer: Lord, we are looking forward to the next age and being with you. Amen

"Mordecai wrote in the name of King Xerxes, sealed the dispatches with the king's signet ring" (Esther 8:10 NIV).

Jesus said, "I [have] come in my Father's name" (John 5:43 KJV).

The disciple Philip asked Jesus to show them the Father; then they would be satisfied. Jesus said that they had seen him, so they had already seen the Father. The Father was in him and he was in the Father. The words and actions Jesus performed were the Father working and speaking through him. (See John 14:8-11.)

Jesus brought glory to God by doing the work that God gave him to do. God will receive glory from our lives if we are doing the works, he has given us to do. As we obey his Word, seek him in prayer and follow the leading of the Spirit, we will fulfill his purposes.

Prayer: Lord, help us to do your will on the earth as Jesus did. Amen

Day 289

"And sent them by mounted couriers, who rode fast horses especially bred for the king" (Esther 8:10 NIV).

"I turned, and lifted up [my] eyes, and looked, and, behold, there came four chariots [and horses] out from between two mountains" (Zechariah 6:1 KJV).

These fast horses of King Xerxes represent the horses and chariots of God.

Zechariah the prophet had a vision of four chariots with horses of different colors: red, black, white and dappled. When Zechariah asked the angel who was there with him what the horses were, he answered that they were the four spirits of the Lord in heaven sent to the earth. (See Zechariah 6:1-5.)

In Revelation 6, we see the purpose of the horses and their riders:

The rider on the white horse was given a bow and was sent to the earth to conquer. The rider on the red horse was given a sword; power was given to him to remove peace from the earth so people would kill each other. The rider on the black horse carried scales to weigh the wheat and barley and was told not to hurt the wine and oil. The rider on the pale horse was named Death and following him was Hell. Power was given to them to kill with the sword, famine and disease—over one fourth of the earth.

Prayer: God, have mercy on your people in the last days. Amen

"The king's edict granted the Jews in every city the right to assemble" (Esther 8:11 NIV).

"Not forsaking the assembling of ourselves together, as the manner of some is" (Hebrews 10:25 KJV).

This verse in Hebrews encourages believers to meet together. When we come together for worship: we can praise the Lord in song, pray, hear the word of God and have fellowship with each other. (See Acts 2:42 for what the early church did when they came together.)

Jesus said, "upon this rock I will build my church" (Matthew 16:18 KJV). Jesus is the Rock the church is built on. "For [no] other foundation can ... man lay than that is laid, which is Jesus Christ" (1 Corinthians 3:11 KJV).

"He is the Rock, his work is perfect ... a God of truth and without iniquity, just and right is he" (Deuteronomy 32:4 KJV). The Israelites in the wilderness, "drank of that spiritual Rock that followed them: and that Rock was Christ" (1 Corinthians 10:4 KJV).

The ultimate reason we gather together is to praise and honor Jesus Christ, the Rock.

Prayer: Lord, when we come together let us remember that honoring you is why we are there. Amen

Day 291

"And protect themselves" (Esther 8:11 NIV).

"Put on the full armor of God, so that you can take your stand against the devil's schemes" (Ephesians 6:11 NIV).

See Ephesians 6:14-18. The armor of God:

The belt of truth: we have the Truth (Christ) wrapped around us; he is our guide. (John 14:6)

The breastplate of righteousness: our hearts are protected by his righteousness. (Philippians 1:11)

Feet: our feet enable us to go and share the gospel with the world. (Isaiah 52:7; 1 Peter 3:15)

The shield of faith: faith puts out the fiery lies the enemy sends our way. (Ephesians 6:16)

The helmet of salvation: it protects our minds from the accusations of the enemy. (Philippians 4:7; Romans 12:2)

The sword of the Spirit: the word of God is our offensive weapon; with it we strike down the enemies of our souls. (Hebrews 4:12)

Prayer: we pray in the power of the Spirit for all of God's children. (Philippians 4:6)

Prayer: Thank you, God, that you provide armor for our protection. Amen

Esther Chapter 8

Day 292

"To destroy, kill and annihilate the armed men of any nationality or province" (Esther 8:11 NIV).

We are in a spiritual battle, a war, but not a war like the world wages. We don't use the weaponry of this world. We have the power of God at our disposal to destroy the hold the devil has over us. (See 2 Corinthians 10:3-4.)

We are to "abstain from fleshly lusts, which war against the soul" (1 Peter 2:11 KJV). Our flesh or sinful nature is at war against our new nature in Christ. Rely on the power of God to have victory over the flesh. (See Romans 7:14-8:14; Colossians 3:5-10, 12-14.)

We war against the devil and evil forces: "we wrestle not against flesh and blood, but against ... the rulers of the darkness of this world, [and] against spiritual wickedness" (Ephesians 6:12 KJV). So what should you do? "Submit yourselves ... to God. Resist the devil, and he will flee from you" (James 4:7 KJV).

We also war against loving worldly things. Pleasing ourselves, wanting whatever we see and boasting about our accomplishments is loving the world. But those who love God and do his will, have life eternally. (See 1 John 2:15-17.) If you are in Christ, "set your affection on things above, not on things on the earth" (Colossians 3:2, KJV).

Prayer: God, be mighty on our behalf and give us victory. Amen

Day 293

"Who might attack them and their women and children, and to plunder the property of their enemies" (Esther 8:11 NIV).

"The Lord will rescue me from every evil attack and will bring me safely to his heavenly kingdom" (2 Timothy 4:18 NIV).

The enemy likes to attack our minds with evil thoughts, fear, doubt, discouragement and many other things. When we realize we are under attack we need to call out to God and ask for his help and deliverance. Philippians 4:6-8 says to pray and ask for God's help and then give him thanks and God's peace will come and protect our hearts and minds. It also tells us to think on things that are true, pure and good.

After we have prayed, we need to redirect our thoughts. Reading or quoting scripture is good; that is what Jesus did when he was tempted. We can also begin to pray for other needs that we know of. We can pray for other believers to stand strong when they are tempted or discouraged.

Also, pray for children who are under attack that they may resist the devil and think and do the right things.

Prayer: Thank you, God, that if we call on you you will come and rescue us. Amen

Day 294

"The day appointed for the Jews to do this in all the provinces of King Xerxes was the thirteenth day of the twelfth month, the month of Adar" (Esther 8:12 NIV).

"He [has] appointed a day, in ... which he will judge the world" (Acts 17:31 KJV).

There is a day appointed for judgment:

"And ... it is appointed unto men once to die, but after this the judgment" (Hebrews 9:27 KJV).

"For we shall all stand before the judgment seat of Christ" and "every one of us shall give account of himself to God" (Romans 14:10, 12 KJV).

"God shall judge the righteous and the wicked" (Ecclesiastes 3:17 KJV).

Jesus said, "Every idle word that men shall speak, they shall give account [of] in the day of judgment" (Matthew 12:36 KJV).

"For the Son of man shall come in the glory of his Father with his angels; and then he shall reward every man according to his works" (Matthew 16:27 KJV). (See also Revelation 11:18.)

Now is the time to be preparing for the day of judgment.

Prayer: Lord, may we prepare for that day by having Christ in our hearts; may our lives be pleasing to you. Amen

Day 295

"A copy of the text of the edict was to be issued as law in every province and made known to the people of every nationality so that the Jews would *be ready on that day to avenge themselves on their enemies*" (Esther 8:13 NIV).

"Vengeance is mine; I will repay," says the Lord. (Romans 12:19 KJV)

God is the one who avenges us and saves us from our enemies. We are not to seek revenge on others when they have offended us. (See Psalm 18:47-48.)

The Lord wants us to forgive others. In Matthew 6:14-15, Jesus says that if we forgive others the Father will also forgive us; but if we don't forgive others he will not forgive us.

Peter once asked Jesus how many times he needed to forgive someone who sinned against him; he suggested seven times, but the Lord said seventy-times-seven times. In other words, we are to forgive any amount, always. We are to forgive as we have been forgiven by Christ. (See Matthew 18:21-22; Ephesians 4:32; Colossians 3:13.)

Prayer: Lord, forgive us as we have forgiven others. Amen (See Matthew 6:12.)

Esther Chapter 8

"The couriers, riding the royal horses, went out, spurred on by the king's command, and the edict was issued in the citadel of Susa" (Esther 8:14 NIV).

"When the powerful horses went out, they were straining to go throughout the earth. And he said, 'Go throughout the earth!' So they went throughout the earth" (Zechariah 6:7 NIV).

Again, in the vision of Zechariah, we see God's horses racing out by his command, to do his will.

Other references to the Lord's horses and chariots:

The prophet Elijah and Elisha were walking along and "there appeared a chariot of fire, and horses of fire, and parted them both ... and Elijah went up by a whirlwind into heaven" (2 Kings 2:11 KJV).

Elisha and his servant saw horses and chariots of fire. (2 Kings 6:17)

"The chariots of God are twenty thousand, even thousands of angels" (Psalm 68:17 KJV).

When the Lamb opens the first four of the seven seals, the different colored horses appear with their riders. Each rider was given an assignment. (Revelation 6:2-8)

The Lord, Faithful and True, is riding a white horse and his army following him is also on white horses. (Revelation 19:11-14)

Prayer: Lord, it will be thrilling to see these fiery chariots and horses someday. Amen

Day 297

"When Mordecai left the king's presence" (Esther 8:15 NIV).

"For the Lord himself shall descend from heaven" (1 Thessalonians 4:16 KJV).

Mordecai leaving the presence of the king represents Jesus leaving the Father to go get his bride.

1 Thessalonians 4:16-17 (KJV) says, "For the Lord himself shall descend from heaven with a shout, with the voice of the archangel, and with the trump of God: and the dead in Christ shall rise first: Then we which are alive and remain shall be caught up together with them in the clouds, to meet the Lord in the air: and so shall we ever be with the Lord." Also, Luke 21:27-28 (KJV): "And then shall they see the Son of Man coming in a cloud with power and great glory. And when these things begin to come to pass, then look up, and lift up your heads; for your redemption [draws near]."

"He was wearing royal garments of blue and white" (Esther 8:15 NIV).

Mordecai's garments match the garden color scheme in Esther 1:6. "My beloved [Christ] is gone down into his garden" (Song of Solomon 6:2 KJV). Again, Christ has gone down to get his bride. (Day 15 tells about the garden being the bride.)

Prayer: Thank you, Jesus, that you are returning for your bride, the church. Amen

"A large crown of gold and a purple robe of fine linen" (Esther 8:15 NIV).

"And the soldiers platted a crown of thorns, and put it on his head, and they put on him a purple robe, And said, Hail, King of the Jews! and they smote him with their hands" (John 19:2-3 KJV).

This happened after Pilate had Jesus beaten, just prior to his crucifixion. The soldiers mocked him by dressing him like a king; with a robe and a crown of thorns on his head. They put a staff in his hand and knelt before him and called him king of the Jews. They spit on him, took the staff and beat him on the head with it. (See Matthew 27:28-30.)

Christ submitted to this humiliation for our sake. "For though he was crucified through weakness, yet he [lives] by the power of God" (2 Corinthians 13:4 KJV).

In the future: "Behold, he [comes] with clouds; and every eye shall see him, and they also which pierced him: and all [tribes] of the earth shall wail because of him. Even so, Amen" (Revelation 1:7 KJV).

Prayer: Lord, the soldiers mockingly called you a king; but someday they will see you as the Almighty King of kings. Amen

Day 299

"And the city of Susa held a joyous celebration" (Esther 8:15 NIV).

"You have come to thousands upon thousands of angels in joyful assembly" (Hebrews 12:22 NIV).

Susa represents heaven. The angels had a joyful assembly when Jesus was born:

There were shepherds in a field outside Bethlehem taking care of flocks of sheep at night. An angel from the Lord appeared before them and God's glory was all around them and they were afraid. The angel told them not to be afraid—he had good news for them and all people. That very day a Savior, the Messiah, had been born in Bethlehem. He was wrapped in cloths and sleeping in a manger. "And suddenly there was with the angel a multitude of the heavenly host praising God, and saying, Glory to God in the highest, and on earth peace, good will toward men" (Luke 2:13-14 KJV). Then the angels returned to heaven.

The shepherds started toward Bethlehem to see the baby that the angel had told them about. They found baby Jesus, Mary and Joseph. After that they went out and told others what they had seen and heard that night. (See Luke 2:8-17.)

Prayer: Thank you, Lord, for the angels who announced your birth. Amen

"For the Jews it was a time of happiness and joy, gladness and honor" (Esther 8:16 NIV).

"Therefore the redeemed of the LORD shall return, and come with singing unto Zion; and everlasting joy shall be upon their head: they shall obtain gladness and joy; and sorrow and mourning shall flee away" (Isaiah 51:11 KJV).

Here is a prophecy concerning the Jews, a future time of happiness and joy:

God said he scattered Israel but will gather them again. He will watch over them like a shepherd watches over his flock. He will deliver them from the hands of their enemies. They will sing for joy and the Lord will bless them with an abundance of grain, wine and oil. They will not have sorrow and sadness any more. Women and men, young and old shall dance and be happy. The Lord will comfort them and turn their sadness into joy. The priests will have plenty and God's people will be filled with the goodness of the Lord. (See Jeremiah 31:10-14.)

Prayer: Lord, bring joy and gladness to your people. May sorrow and suffering be a thing of the past. Amen

Day 301

"In every province and in every city to which the edict of the king came, *there was joy and gladness among the Jews, with feasting and celebrating*" (Esther 8:17 NIV).

"Rejoice in the Lord always. I will say it again: Rejoice!" (Philippians 4:4 NIV).

What if there isn't a feast and much of a reason to celebrate? Could we still rejoice in the Lord?

Consider this scenario from Habakkuk 3:17:

The fig trees in the orchard didn't bloom—which means there won't be any fruit.

The grapevine shriveled and now there are no grapes to sell.

The olive trees failed to produce olives.

The crops got burned up by the summer heat. There won't be a harvest this year.

The sheep got loose and now they are nowhere to be found.

The cattle contracted a disease and had to be put down.

"Yet I will rejoice in the LORD, I will joy in the God of my salvation. The LORD God is my strength" (Habakkuk 3:18-19 KJV).

Prayer: Lord, help us to rejoice in you even in the bad times. Amen

"And many people of other nationalities became Jews because fear of the Jews had seized them" (Esther 8:17 NIV).

"Great fear came upon all the church, and upon as many as heard these things" (Acts 5:11 KJV).

In Acts 5:1-11, there is a story about a man named Ananias and his wife Saphira. They sold land and kept part of the money. The rest Ananias gave to the apostles to help those in need. Peter asked Ananias why he had listened to Satan and lied by saying he gave all of the money from the sale. (The money was his to do with as he wanted, but the wrong part was in saying he brought all the money for the apostles.) Peter told him he had lied to God, not just to people. Immediately Ananias dropped dead. Everyone who heard about this became afraid.

A little while later Saphira, his wife came in. Peter asked her about the money for the land and she lied to him as Ananias had done. She also dropped dead and they buried her beside her husband. The church and all who heard about this were afraid.

Prayer: Lord, may all the earth fear and respect you. May they call out to you for mercy. Amen

Day 303

Chapter 8 Review

Day 270: Christ came because we needed the power of God to change our hearts.

Day 272: Lord, you are all powerful; nothing is too hard for you.

Day 274: We plead for the Lord to come and put an end to the evil in the world.

Day 275: God has provided the way (Jesus) with directions (the Bible) so that we can reach our destination (heaven) safely and on time.

Day 276: After having prayed and obeyed—stand.

Day 282: God's name is "I AM". I am your provider. I am your salvation. I am your deliverer. I am your healer. I am your Father. I am your everything.

Day 290: We come together as the church to praise and honor Jesus Christ.

Day 295: We are to forgive as we have been forgiven by Christ.

Prayer: Lord, may we put our trust in the great and powerful I AM. Amen

Esther Chapter 8

Day 304

Chapter 8 Challenge

Answer the questions below.

1. King Xerxes gave something to Queen Esther that was Haman's. What was it? (8:1)

2. What did Esther reveal to the king about Mordecai? (8:1)

3. The king gave something important to Mordecai. What was it? (8:2)

4. What position did Esther bestow on Mordecai? (8:2)

5. Esther pleaded with the king to do what for her and her people? (8:3-5)

6. Who wrote out the new orders in the name of the king? (8:10)

7. The new edict granted the Jews the right to do what? (8:11, 13)

8. Why did many people become Jews at this time? (8:17)

Prayer: Thank you, Lord, that you are able to rescue your people from their enemies. Amen

Day 305

"On the thirteenth day of the twelfth month, the month of Adar, *the edict commanded by the king was to be carried out*" (Esther 9:1 NIV).

"Therefore shall [you] keep my commandments, and do them: I am the LORD" (Leviticus 22:31 KJV).

When an earthly king gives a command, he expects it to be carried out; how much more should the heavenly King's orders be heeded.

Jesus said that obeying his commands shows that we love him, and if we love him, the Father will love us as well. Jesus, too, will love us and reveal himself to us. Obeying his commands keeps us in the shelter of his love. In the same way, Jesus obeyed the Father's commands and remained in his love. We are commanded to love each other just as he loves us.

We are his friends if we do what he commands us to do. (See John 14:21, 15:10-12, 14.)

Prayer: Lord, help us to obey your commands; that shows we love you. Amen

"On this day the enemies of the Jews had hoped to overpower them, but now the tables were turned and the Jews got the upper hand over those who hated them" (Esther 9:1 NIV).

"You give us victory over our enemies, and put our adversaries to shame" (Psalm 44:7 NIV).

Here are other promises of God that assure us that he is greater than the enemies who come against us:

"I will call upon the LORD, who is worthy to be praised: so shall I be saved from [my] enemies" (Psalm 18:3 KJV).

"[You] are of God, little children, and have overcome them: because greater is he that is in you, than he that is in the world" (1 John 4:4 KJV).

Our part is to call to God for help, obey him, and trust him to carry us through the temptation or trouble. We need to be patient; he doesn't often immediately work a miracle; mostly he delivers us step by step. We need to keep our faith in God. Faith is believing God is working on our behalf, even when we don't see it or feel it. Hang on and speak his Word as truth in the situation. He is faithful.

Prayer: God, you are greater than our enemies; may we trust you. Amen

Day 307

"The Jews assembled in their cities in all the provinces of King Xerxes" (Esther 9:2 NIV).

"Many were gathered together praying" (Acts 12:12 KJV).

The Jews being assembled represents believers gathered together to pray.

King Herod had Peter arrested and put in prison. The church was passionately praying for him to be released. The night before he was to be tried, Peter was awakened by an angel of the Lord. The angel told him to get dressed and follow him. Peter thought he was having a vision. But it was real. The angel led Peter past the guards and out the gate, which opened for them automatically. A short time later the angel left.

Then Peter went to the house of Mary, where the disciples were praying for him. He knocked on the door and a girl came. She recognized his voice and went in to tell the group Peter was there. In her excitement she forgot to let him in. They didn't believe her and said it was his angel. Peter kept knocking and finally he was let in. The people there were amazed at the power of God. (See Acts 12:1-16.)

Prayer: Thank you Lord; you hear and answer the prayers of your church. Amen

Esther Chapter 9

"To attack those determined to destroy them" (Esther 9:2 NIV).

"The prayer of a righteous person is powerful and effective" (James 5:16 NIV).

We have a powerful force to use against those determined to destroy us: prayer!

Joshua and his army went to fight in a battle and the Lord was with them. Joshua prayed that the sun would stay up so they could continue to fight their enemies. "And the sun stood still ... until the people had avenged themselves upon their enemies. ... And there was no day like that before it or after it ... for the LORD fought for Israel" (Joshua 10:13-14 KJV).

When Paul and Silas were in prison; they prayed and sang songs of praise to God. "And suddenly there was a great earthquake, so that the foundations of the prison were shaken: and immediately all the doors were opened, and every one's bands were loosed" (Acts 16:25-26 KJV). Paul and Silas were released.

Prayer: Lord, you are a mighty God. Amen

Day 309

"No one could stand against them" (Esther 9:2 NIV).

"No one will be able to stand against you" (Deuteronomy 11:25 NIV).

God told the Israelites that if they loved and served him with all their hearts and did not worship other gods, he would give them victory over their enemies. If they would obey his commands, no one could stop them from possessing the land the Lord had promised them. All these blessings were contingent on whether they fully obeyed him.

Think about God's promises and commands. Teach your children his Word. Talk about the Lord at home, on the road, when you get up and when you go to bed. Write his words down and post them around your house. (See Deuteronomy 11:18-25.)

The stories in the Bible are there so we can learn from them. If we want God's special blessing, we need to obey him. And if we want power over the enemy, we have to obey God and be faithful to the Lord in the day-to-day walk of life.

Prayer: Lord, when we obey you, you drive out our enemies so we can live our lives pleasing to you. Amen

"Because the people of all the other nationalities were afraid of them" (Esther 9:2 NIV).

"For the LORD your God shall lay the fear of you and the dread of you upon all the land" (Deuteronomy 11:25 KJV).

The Lord promised Israel victory over their enemies if they obeyed his commands. That is why the enemies feared them—because with God on their side they were unstoppable.

We can walk in victory over our enemies if we obey his commands. This cannot be stressed enough. God loves us and has compassion on us and wants good for us, but he wants us to obey him.

Jesus said, "If any man will come after me, let him deny himself, and take up his cross daily, and follow me" (Luke 9:23 KJV). Following him requires us to deny "self" which is difficult; we like to have our own way. We need to die to our selfish desires daily or we can become lazy and complacent. The Apostle Paul said, "I die daily" (1 Corinthians 15:31 KJV).

If all of God's people were to consistently obey him, we would be a force to be reckoned with. It wouldn't be anything of ourselves; it would be the power of God working through his church.

Prayer: God, help us to die to "self" so we can live for you. Amen

Day 311

"And all the nobles of the provinces, the satraps, the governors and the king's administrators helped the Jews, *because fear of Mordecai had seized them*" (Esther 9:3 NIV).

"By mercy and truth iniquity is purged: and by the fear of the Lord men depart from evil" (Proverbs 16:6 KJV).

God is the only one we are to fear. We are in awe of his mighty power. He is creator and sustainer of the universe. He is big and powerful, yet personal enough to know our thoughts and plans. We have a reverent fear of him because we will someday stand before him to give account of our lives on this earth. Those who are Christ's can stand in his righteousness on that day. As for those not in Christ, may they learn to fear God now and turn to him for forgiveness and be washed clean.

"Let us hear the conclusion of the whole matter: Fear God, and keep his commandments: for this is the whole duty of man" (Ecclesiastes 12:13 KJV).

Prayer: Lord, may we have a healthy fear of you, so that pleasing you is our top priority. Amen

Esther Chapter 9

Day 312

"Mordecai was prominent in the palace" (Esther 9:4 NIV).

"[Christ] is "worthy to take the book, and to open the seals" (Revelation 5:9 KJV).

Mordecai was great in the king's palace, as Christ is great in heaven.

In the Apostle John's vision of heaven, an angel is calling out in a loud voice asking, "Who is worthy to open the book, and to loose the seals?" (Revelation 5:2 KJV). But no one was found worthy—in heaven or on the earth. John began to weep because no one was worthy to open the book and read it. Then an elder in heaven told John not to weep because the Lion of the tribe of Judah was found worthy to break the seals and open the book.

Four heavenly beings and twenty-four elders sang this song: You, (the Lamb) are worthy to take the book and open the seals because you were killed, and your blood bought people for God from every tribe and nation. And they will serve God and reign as kings and priests on the earth. (See Revelation 5.)

"Blessing, and [honor], and glory, and power, be unto him that [sits on] the throne, and unto the Lamb for ever and ever" (Revelation 5:13 KJV).

Prayer: Jesus, you are great. We love and worship you. Amen

Day 313

"[Mordecai's] reputation spread throughout the provinces" (Esther 9:4 NIV).

"News about [Jesus] spread through the whole countryside" (Luke 4:14 NIV).

Jesus went out healing many people of diseases and sicknesses. Sometimes after Jesus healed people, he told them not to tell anyone. But often they went around the town and told what had happened to them. Because of this, Jesus couldn't enter a town without being mobbed. So he traveled through the deserted countryside, but still people found him. They came from all over the region to see him and have their needs met. (See Matthew 15:30-31.)

Even the ruler Herod, had heard about Jesus and hoped to see him perform a miracle. (See Luke 23:8.)

Prayer: Jesus, may your church tell others the wonderful things that you do. Amen

"And [Mordecai] became more and more powerful" (Esther 9:4 NIV).

"Jesus returned to Galilee in the power of the Spirit" (Luke 4:14 NIV).

The people "were all amazed at the mighty power of God" that was at work through Jesus. (Luke 9:43 KJV) He raised the dead, calmed storms, multiplied food to feed thousands and cast out demons and did many other great wonders.

When Jesus was questioned by Pilate, he remained silent. Pilate didn't like that Jesus refused to answer him. He told him he had the power to free him or crucify him. Jesus told Pilate he only had that power because it was given to him from above. (See John 19:7-11.)

Jesus could have used his power to destroy his enemies, but he didn't. While on the cross he said, "Father, forgive them, for they do not know what they are doing" (Luke 23:34 NIV). He loved his enemies and forgave them.

Prayer: Jesus, thank you for the power of your love. Amen

Day 315

"The Jews struck down all their enemies with the sword, killing and destroying them, and they did what they pleased to those who hated them" (Esther 9:5 NIV).

"And take ... the sword of the Spirit, which is the word of God" (Ephesians 6:17 KJV).

The weapon God equips us with to strike down our enemies is the sword of the Spirit, God's word.

"For the word of God is quick, and powerful, and sharper than any [two-edged] sword, piercing even to the dividing asunder of soul and spirit, and of the joints and marrow, and is a discerner of the thoughts and intents of the heart" (Hebrews 4:12 KJV).

God's word is powerful. Jesus used the Scriptures to fight the devil when he was tempted in the desert. Live in Christ and let his words live in you. (See John 15:7.) Believing and acting on the word of God gives us victory in our lives and changes us into people God can use to expand his kingdom on the earth.

Prayer: Lord, may your Word be in our hearts and on our minds, so we are prepared to face our enemies and have victory over them. Amen

Esther Chapter 9

"In the citadel of Susa" (Esther 9:6 NIV).

"[You] shall see heaven open, and the angels of God ascending and descending upon the Son of Man" (John 1:51 KJV).

As humans, we don't see the invisible spiritual activity that is going on around us in our world and in the heavens. But sometimes God lets people get a glimpse. In a dream, Jacob saw a ladder reaching up to heaven; and the angels of God were going up and down the ladder. At the top stood the Lord, who spoke to Jacob and told him he would take care of him. (See Genesis 28:11-15.)

An angel of the Lord appeared to Joseph in a dream to tell him that Mary's baby, was from the Holy Spirit. And an angel appeared to him again after the wise men had brought their gifts. The angel told Joseph to take Mary and her child and go to Egypt because Herod wanted to kill Jesus. (See Matthew 1:20, 2:13.)

Hebrew 13:2 (KJV) says, we should "entertain strangers: for ... some have entertained angels unawares." You don't know, sometime you may help a stranger and it's an angel and you aren't even aware of it. God's ways are mysterious.

Prayer: Lord, you are God over the things that are seen as well as things unseen. Amen

Day 317

"The Jews killed and destroyed five hundred men" (Esther 9:6 NIV).

"Knowing this, that our old [self] is crucified with him, that the body of sin might be destroyed, that [from now on] we should not serve sin" (Romans 6:6 KJV).

If Christ is to be at work through us, our sinful nature must first be destroyed. It's only in his strength that we resist sin and live holy lives.

"I am crucified with Christ: nevertheless I live; yet not I, but Christ [lives] in me: and the life which I now live in the flesh I live by the faith of the Son of God, who loved me, and gave himself for me" (Galatians 2:20 KJV).

With Christ in us, we can live Spirit-led lives like Jesus lived when he walked on this earth. (Except we won't walk it perfectly like he did.) He wants us to be "sons of God" on the earth. Are we giving Christ enough control to live his life through us?

Prayer: Lord, help us to yield to you and do your will. Amen

In the next few verses (9:7-9) we see the ten sons of Haman whom the Jews killed. The scriptures quoted show how these evil kings followed in the footsteps of their evil fathers and forefathers.

"[The Jews killed] Parshandatha, and Dalphon, and Aspatha" (Esther 9:7 KJV).

"And he did that which was evil in the sight of the LORD, as his fathers had done" (2 Kings 15:9 KJV). Fathers have a big influence on their children, especially their sons.

"And Poratha, and Adalia, and Aridatha" (Esther 9:8 KJV).

"[Amon] did that which was evil in the sight of the LORD, as his father Manasseh did" (2 Kings 21:20 KJV). Fathers are to be the earthly representatives of the heavenly Father; when they fail in this, it is a great loss and detriment to the family.

"And Parmashta, and Arisai, and Aridai and Vajezatha" (Esther 9:9 KJV).

"[Abijah] committed all the sins his father had done before him" (1 Kings 15:3 NIV). If the father is doing evil; he is setting a pattern for his children to follow. Their only hope of restoration and freedom from evil is in Christ.

Prayer: Lord, we pray for fathers to be saved: to live holy lives, and to be role models of godly living for their children. Amen

Day 319

"The ten sons of Haman son of Hammedatha, the enemy of the Jews" (Esther 9:10 NIV).

"[You] are of your father the devil" (John 8:44 KJV).

Haman represents the devil and the ten sons the devil's offspring.

Some Jews, who didn't believe in Jesus, claimed that God was their Father, but their actions proved them wrong. Jesus told them that their father was the devil. (See John 8:42-44.)

May we who claim that God is our Father live in a way that shows we are followers of his Son, Jesus. "The LORD is merciful and gracious, slow to anger, and plenteous in mercy" (Psalm 103:8 KJV). Are we being merciful and gracious to others? Or are we quick to get angry when things don't go our way. Let's be like our Father and show mercy and patience with others. Being a control freak can make us angry and impatient with people. We need to give the Lord control of our lives, and let God be "God" in other people's lives, not us.

Prayer: Lord, you are merciful and patient with us. May you give us grace to show mercy and patience to others. Amen

Esther Chapter 9

"But they did not lay their hands on the plunder" (Esther 9:10 NIV).

"For we brought nothing into this world, and it is certain we can carry nothing out" (1 Timothy 6:7 KJV).

We may start with nothing and leave with nothing, but in between we can accumulate a lot: things that need to be dusted, stored, repaired or insured; and left behind when we down-size, or die. If we have things we don't need, or are not using, we could pass them on to someone else.

Jesus said, "Take heed, and beware of covetousness: for a man's life [consists] not in the abundance of the things which he [possesses]" (Luke 12:15 KJV).

Prayer: Lord, help us to let go of stuff we don't need, so we can be freer to serve you. Amen

Day 321

"The number of those killed in the citadel of Susa *was reported to the king that same day*" (Esther 9:11 NIV).

"And the seventy [disciples of Jesus] returned again with joy, saying, Lord, even the devils are subject unto us through [your] name" (Luke 10:17 KJV). (The disciples were reporting back to Jesus what they had done.)

Jesus warned his disciples not to rejoice in successful ministry, "but rather rejoice, because your names are written in heaven" (Luke 10:20 KJV).

Success can be dangerous to our souls. We must be careful to give God the glory, in our hearts and before others, so that we don't get puffed up in pride. Even the Apostle Paul was given a thorn in the flesh to keep him from being proud of the many visions and revelations the Lord had given him. (See 2 Corinthians 12:7.)

Prayer: Lord, may we walk humbly before you. Amen

"The king said to Queen Esther" (Esther 9:12 NIV).

"What I say to you, I say to everyone: 'Watch!'" (Mark 13:37 NIV).

In one parable, Jesus told about a man in a high position who was going far away on a trip. He left his workers with jobs to do and the authority to carry them out. One of them was assigned to keep watch; they didn't know when the boss would return. They didn't want to be found sleeping and unprepared. We don't know when the Lord will return, so we need to be watching and ready for him. (See Mark 13:34-37.)

We can watch for the Lord's coming in the future but also be aware how he may come during our day. He may come wanting us to do something. We need to watch for opportunities from the Lord to pray, call, visit or help someone. We can be an answer to someone's prayer.

We need to pray and watch out so that we don't fall into sin; our spirit is willing to obey God but our flesh fails easily. (See Matthew 26:41).

Prayer: Lord, may we watch for you today and be available when you need us to do something. Amen

Day 323

"The Jews have killed and destroyed five hundred men and the ten sons of Haman in the citadel of Susa. *What have they done in the rest of the king's provinces?*" (Esther 9:12 NIV).

"The Lord ... sent them ... to every town" (Luke 10:1 NIV).

The Lord sent out seventy disciples to go to the towns where he was planning to go. Jesus told them there were few workers even though the harvest was great. He said for them to pray to God for more workers to go and harvest the crop. (See Luke 10:1-2). The Lord still needs laborers for his harvest field, the world.

We need to pray for missionaries who have left all—family, friends and country to take the gospel around the world. They need our financial help as well. We can also show our support by attending a meeting where they tell about the work they are doing.

There are many well-established and worthy Christian ministries that help the needy and share the gospel. We can partner with them by praying and giving.

Those who share the gospel on the home front need our prayers as well. Our local churches have ministries; we can join them and help harvest a crop for the Lord.

Prayer: Lord, send out workers for the harvest of lost souls. Amen

"Now what is your petition? It will be given you. What is your request? It will also be granted" (Esther 9:12 NIV).

"If [you] shall ask any thing in my name, I will do it" (John 14:14 KJV).

When we ask in Jesus' name, we take into consideration his character and his revealed will as expressed in the word of God, the Bible. For example, don't ask God to help you steal a car you've been wanting. He has already told us not to steal, in the Ten Commandments. (See Exodus 20:15.) He wouldn't answer that request because it goes against his character, will and purposes.

We can pray he would provide us a car, if it is his will. He may have someone give us a car; or he may give us an idea how to earn extra money so we can save up for a car. When we pray for something, God can answer our prayers in a way we hadn't thought about. Or his answer may be that we don't need a car right now. Then we need to be patient and wait on his timing. (A car is just an example. Replace the word car with whatever you want the Lord to provide for you.)

Prayer: Lord, when we ask for something, may we be open to the way you want to answer—then we won't be disappointed. Amen

Day 325

"'If it pleases the king,' Esther answered, 'give the Jews in Susa permission to *carry out this day's edict* tomorrow also, and let Haman's ten sons be impaled on poles'" (Esther 9:13 NIV).

"Today, if you hear his voice, do not harden your hearts" (Hebrews 3:7-8 NIV).

Today we can: pray or not, obey or not, thank God or not, be kind or not, forgive or not.

Today, we will enjoy the benefits of yesterday's good choices and/or suffer the consequences of the bad decisions we have made.

Today is the only day we have to give the Lord.

Yesterday's gone, and we can't change what happened.

Tomorrow isn't guaranteed.

Today is the most important day of our lives:

Today, we can pray and ask the Lord for forgiveness; today, we can make that phone call; today, we can be kind and loving with the Lord's help; and today, we can make good choices as we follow his leading.

"Choose you this day whom [you] will serve" (Joshua 24:15 KJV).

Prayer: Lord, help us to live for you today! Amen

"So the king commanded that this be done. An edict was issued in Susa, and they impaled the ten sons of Haman" (Esther 9:14 NIV).

God commanded that this was to be done: "Go and ... utterly destroy all" (1 Samuel 15:3 KJV).

In 1 Samuel 15, the prophet Samuel told King Saul, that the Lord had commanded him to fight the Amalekites and wipe them out, destroying everything. So Saul and his army attacked the Amalekites, but spared the king and the best of the flocks. When Samuel saw what Saul had done, he rebuked him. Saul's excuse was that he wanted to save the animals to sacrifice to the Lord. But Samuel told him that the Lord was more interested in obedience than sacrifices. "To obey is better than sacrifice" (1 Samuel 15:22 KJV). For his disobedience, Saul was rejected by God as king.

Often the sacrifices we make are good—we sacrifice one thing to gain something better. But to give up something "for the Lord" in the hope that we won't have to do the thing he really wants us to do won't work with him. For God "shows no partiality and accepts no bribes" (Deuteronomy 10:17 NIV).

Prayer: Lord, help us to obey you in all things. Amen

Day 327

"The Jews in Susa came together on the fourteenth day of the month of Adar" (Esther 9:15 NIV).

"We ... are compassed about with so great a cloud of witnesses" (Hebrews 12:1 KJV).

The Jews in Susa represent the believers in heaven: the great cloud of witnesses.

Since we have a cloud of witnesses; we should rid ourselves of anything that slows us down and the sin that trips us up in our pursuit of Jesus. With patient endurance we should run the race he has purposed for us, looking to him as our example. He endured the pain and humiliation of the cross knowing there was joy ahead, and he is now sitting at the right hand of God. (See Hebrews 12:1-2.)

Just as Jesus and the saints before us were faithful to God, so the Lord is with us to help us to remain faithful to him. (See Hebrews 11.)

Prayer: Lord, help us in running "the race." Amen

"And they put to death" (Esther 9:15 NIV).

"Put to death, therefore, whatever belongs to your earthly nature: sexual immorality, impurity, lust, evil desires and greed, which is idolatry" (Colossians 3:5 NIV).

If we want to live the Christian life we must, by the help of the Holy Spirit, put to death the sinful deeds we are prone to do, because we will die spiritually if we continue in them. Those who obey the leading of the Spirit are truly the Lord's people. (See Romans 8:13-14.)

We need to put to death our independent streak and be ruled by God, not ruled by self. When self is on the throne, it does what it wants when it wants. Pride, one of the deadliest sins, is the product of a self-ruled life; it thinks it knows best. The truth is, God knows best.

Prayer: Lord, help us to put to death any sins in our lives and submit wholly to you. Amen

Day 329

"In Susa *three hundred men*" (Esther 9:15 NIV).

"And the LORD said unto Gideon, By the three hundred men ... will I save you, and deliver the Midianites into [your] hand" (Judges 7:7 KJV).

At this time, the Lord was punishing the Israelites by allowing the Midianites to oppress them. (They again had forgotten the Lord and were worshiping false gods.) The Midianites would come and destroy their crops and take their animals. The Israelites were so distressed they called out to the Lord to help them.

Gideon was called by the Lord to deliver the Israelites. He gathered an army and assembled it for battle. The Lord told Gideon his army was too big; when God gave them the victory, they would take the credit. Under the Lord's direction, Gideon thinned out over thirty thousand men. God saved them from their enemies with only three hundred men. (See Judges 6-7.)

The victory over our enemies isn't about the size of our army, resources, strength, knowledge or money. The LORD gives us victory over our enemies.

Prayer: Lord, deliver us from our enemies; our trust is in you alone. Amen

"But they did not lay their hands on the plunder" (Esther 9:15 NIV).

"For the love of money is the root of all evil" (1 Timothy 6:10 KJV).

Be careful, if your goal in life is to be rich; you may find yourself in all kinds of tempting situations that will bring you down. Some believers who chased after money have left the faith and become miserable. Church, don't get caught in that trap. Flee! Instead, pursue faith, love, humility and a godly life. Fight for your faith—hold on, and you will gain eternal life. That's what you were called to.

If you are rich, don't be proud or trust in your riches, but trust in God, who will provide for you. Instead, be rich in good deeds and give to those in need. In doing this you will lay a strong foundation for the next life—in eternity. (See 1 Timothy 6:9-12, 17-19.)

Prayer: Lord, may we pursue faith, love and righteousness, not earthly riches. Amen

Day 331

"Meanwhile, the remainder of the Jews who were in the king's provinces also *assembled to protect themselves and get relief from their enemies*" (Esther 9:16 NIV).

"When you are assembled ... the power of our Lord Jesus is present" (1 Corinthians 5:4 NIV). "For where two or three are gathered together in my name, there I am in the midst of them" (Matthew 18:20 KJV).

When we as believers come together and worship the Lord, there is spiritual relief from the enemies of our souls. This is especially true for those in difficult circumstances: those who live with unbelievers, for example, or those who face persecution. They can find an "oasis in the desert" when they gather with other Christians. The Lord is there to refresh them, and their brothers and sisters in Christ are there to encourage them.

In his letter to the Thessalonians, Paul rejoiced that the believers were enduring hardships patiently and keeping their faith in the midst of trials and persecutions. He assured them that God would give them relief from the enemies who were causing them so much trouble. When Christ returns, the wicked will be punished. (See 2 Thessalonians 1:4-9.)

Prayer: Lord, be with us as we come together and give us relief from our enemies. Amen

"They killed seventy-five thousand of them *but did not lay their hands on the plunder*" (Esther 9:16 NIV).

"For where your treasure is, there will your heart be also" (Matthew 6:21 KJV).

Don't accumulate lots of treasures here on earth; they don't last, and they might get stolen. Instead, stock up on heavenly treasures; they don't attract thieves. Your heart is involved in whatever you treasure, so choose carefully. A person can only serve one master: his love and devotion will go to his treasures, or his love and devotion will go to God. (See Matthew 6:19-21, 24.)

Storing up treasure on earth is about getting; storing up treasure in heaven is about giving. Now is a good time to start storing up treasure in heaven. We can give love, mercy, an encouraging word, the gospel, food, money, time—the list could go on and on.

Prayer: Lord, you are the greatest treasure in this world. May we share your love with others by giving whatever we can. Amen

Day 333

"This happened on the thirteenth day of the month of Adar, and on the fourteenth *they rested*" (Esther 9:17 NIV).

"Come with me by yourselves to a quiet place and get some rest" (Mark 6:31 NIV).

Jesus told his disciples to come away from the crowds and get some rest; the disciples hadn't even had time to eat because of all the people coming for help. We also need to get away somewhere quiet and alone with Jesus to get rest for our bodies and souls.

When one or more parts of the body are neglected the other parts suffer as well. The body functions best when it gets proper rest, nutritional food, exercise and adequate shelter. The soul finds rest in submitting to Christ (See Matthew 11:28-30.) The spirit that joins with the Holy Spirit finds rest as it communes with God. (See 1 Corinthians 6:17.)

Prayer: "[May the] God of peace sanctify you wholly; and I pray [to] God [that] your whole spirit and soul and body be preserved blameless unto the coming of our Lord Jesus Christ" (1 Thessalonians 5:23 KJV). Amen

Day 334

"And made it a day of feasting and joy" (Esther 9:17 NIV).
"A feast is made for laughter" (Ecclesiastes 10:19 KJV).

What fun we have when family or friends come together for food and fellowship, especially when we share the same faith in Christ. Whether it's a feast at Thanksgiving with relatives or a picnic in the yard with your kids—enjoy!

The Lord planned days of feasting in the Jewish calendar year. These feasts were days off from their regular work and involved giving an offering to the Lord. The offering might be grain from the fields or a lamb from the flocks. The purpose of the celebrations was to remind the people of everything the Lord had done for them. (See Leviticus 23 for a list of the different holy feasts.)

The Christian church celebrates holy times during the year for the same reason: so we won't forget what the Lord has done for us. We celebrate the Lord's birth, his death and his resurrection, usually with special meals or programs.

Prayer: Thank you, Lord, that we have special times to remember you. Amen

Day 335

"The Jews in Susa, however, had assembled on the thirteenth and fourteenth, and then on the fifteenth *they rested*" (Esther 9:18 NIV).

"Anyone who enters God's rest also rests from their works" (Hebrews 4:10 NIV).

A soul that is at rest is one that is totally surrendered to God's will. If we are resting in God, we have stopped doing "our" works: stopped doing things our way.

A father's walk with his child can be a restful excursion if the child holds the father's hand or walks beside him peacefully. When a child tugs on the father's hand and tries to pull him in a different direction, or runs ahead into the street—that is not the definition of rest.

Can we rest in our Father's arms and let him carry us where he wishes?

Prayer: Father, may we rest in you and not struggle against your will for us. Amen

Day 336

"And made it a day of feasting and joy" (Esther 9:18 NIV).

"He provides you with plenty of food and fills your hearts with joy" (Acts 14:17 NIV).

We are blessed; let's continually thank the Lord for providing for us—for physical blessings and spiritual blessings.

Praise to God from Psalm 103:1-5: I will give praise to the Lord with all my heart and soul. I won't forget to thank him for all his benefits. He forgives my sins and heals my sicknesses. He protects my life. The Lord pours out his love and mercy on me richly. He provides good things for me to eat so my strength is renewed.

You can rejoice "for the joy of the LORD is your strength" (Nehemiah 8:10 KJV). "A merry heart [has] a continual feast" (Proverbs 15:15 KJV).

Prayer: Thank you, God, for food to eat and joy in our hearts. Amen

Day 337

"That is why rural Jews—those living in villages—observe the fourteenth of the month of Adar as a day of joy and feasting, a day for *giving presents to each other*" (Esther 9:19 NIV).

"Now concerning spiritual gifts ... I would not have you ignorant" (1 Corinthians 12:1 KJV).

The presents represent the "gifts" of the Holy Spirit.

There are different gifts all from the same Holy Spirit. The gifts of the Spirit are to build up the body of Christ; each member has something to contribute to the whole body. Just as there are different ways to serve and help others in the practical realm, there are spiritual gifts to help others by the supernatural working of the Spirit.

Some of the gifts are faith, words of wisdom and knowledge, gifts of healing and the working of miracles. (See 1 Corinthians 12:1-11.) Jesus was led by the Spirit and we can read about the gifts at work in him in the gospels. (Matthew, Mark, Luke and John.)

There are stories in the Bible of the Spirit coming on people and enabling them to do miraculous things or know things because God told them. God's spirit has always been at work—even in creation. (See Genesis 1:2.)

Prayer: Lord, may your people allow the Spirit to work through them to do your will. Amen

Esther Chapter 9

"Mordecai recorded these events, and he sent letters to all the Jews throughout the provinces of King Xerxes, near and far" (Esther 9:20 NIV).

"And they wrote letters" (Acts 15:23 KJV).

These letters Mordecai sent represent the New Testament.

The New Testament of the Bible is the written record we have of the events in the life of Jesus (The Books of Matthew through John) and the early church (The Book of Acts).

The Books of Romans through Jude were letters written to specific churches or to individuals. The Apostle Paul wrote most of these letters. They reveal more about God the Father, Jesus and the Holy Spirit. They also give instructions for church government and for living the Christian life.

The last book of the New Testament, the Book of Revelation, is the revelation of Jesus Christ given to the Apostle John. It contains letters to different churches and words of prophecy.

God gave us these letters, and the whole Bible, so that we might know Him.

Prayer: Lord, may we read and study your Word so we may know you better. Amen

Day 339

"To have them celebrate annually the fourteenth and fifteenth days of the month of Adar" (Esther 9:21 NIV).

"[He] went up out of his city yearly to worship" (1 Samuel 1:3 KJV).

Mordecai told the Jews to celebrate their victory over their enemies every year.

We celebrate Christ's death and resurrection (Easter) every year. Christ was victorious over his enemies; because of his victory, we too have victory over our enemies—sin and death!

This is the gospel presented in short form:

Christ died and rose
To sin dispose
That we may be
Forever free

Prayer: Thank you Jesus for saving us from our enemies—now and forever. Amen

"As the time when the Jews got relief from their enemies" (Esther 9:22 NIV).

"That we being delivered out of the hand of our enemies might serve him without fear" (Luke 1:74 KJV).

It is through Christ that we can get relief and deliverance from our enemies—sin and death. "Now [we are] being made free from sin, and [have] become servants to God" (Romans 6:22 KJV). In him, we will be made holy and have the promise of eternal life. We have been set free from sin, not to look better in the eyes of others, or to feel better about ourselves, but to live holy lives before God and do his will.

We don't have to look far to see the damaging effects of sin—in our lives, in our families, in our communities and in our world. Jesus is the only one who can save, heal and deliver us, our families and our world. Only he can give us real hope—and not just hope, but we attain what we have hoped for: peace, love, security, family and a good future. (See Jeremiah 29:11.)

Prayer: Free us, Lord, so that we may love and serve you. Amen

Day 341

"And as the month when *their sorrow was turned into joy and their mourning into a day of celebration*" (Esther 9:22 NIV).

"And they departed quickly from the sepulcher with fear and great joy; and did run to bring his disciples word" (Matthew 28:8 KJV).

The disciples' sorrow (Jesus' death) was turned into joy because Jesus was no longer in the tomb—he was alive.

When Jesus appeared to his disciples, the disciple Thomas wasn't there. When Thomas heard about it later, he said he wouldn't believe it was really Jesus unless he saw the nail scars in his hands and feet. A week later, Thomas was there when Jesus appeared again. Jesus told Thomas to reach out touch his hands and side, and believe. Jesus said that Thomas believed because he saw him with his own eyes; but "blessed are they that have not seen, and yet have believed" (John 20:29 KJV).

Later, Jesus was seen by five hundred people all at once. (See 1 Corinthians 15:6.) For forty days he was with them, telling them about the kingdom of God. Then he returned to his Father in heaven. (See Acts 1:3.)

Prayer: Lord, may many come to believe in you even though they can't see you. Amen

"He wrote them to observe the days as days of feasting and joy and *giving presents of food to one another and gifts to the poor*" (Esther 9:22 NIV).

"I was hungry and you gave me something to eat ... I needed clothes and you clothed me" (Matthew 25:35-36 NIV).

Jesus said that when he sits on his throne in heaven and it is time for the nations to stand before him, the people will be separated the way a shepherd separates the sheep from the goats. The righteous will inherit the kingdom God has prepared for them.

Jesus used this example: when he was hungry, thirsty or needed clothing, the righteous provided for him. And when he was sick and in prison, they visited him. They asked Jesus, when did they see him hungry, sick or in prison? Jesus answered, "As [you] have done it unto one of the least of these ... [you] have done it unto me" (Matthew 25:40 KJV). These people would inherit the kingdom of God. In other words, those who do for others in need as they would for Christ will be rewarded by the Father with eternal life. Those who ignore the needy will be punished eternally. (See Matthew 25:31-46.)

Prayer: Lord, help us to see the needs around us and respond. Amen

Day 343

"So the Jews agreed to continue the celebration they had begun" (Esther 9:23 NIV).

"Do this in remembrance of me" (Luke 22:19 NIV).

Jesus was eating with his twelve disciples one last time when "he took bread, and gave thanks, and [broke] it, and gave unto them, saying, This is my body which is given for you: this do in remembrance of me. Likewise [he] also [took] the cup after supper, saying, This cup is the new testament in my blood, which is shed for you'" (Luke 22:19-20 KJV).

Today believers everywhere continue to celebrate Holy Communion as Jesus commanded. This is done so we can remember and be thankful for all that Christ did for us on the cross.

It would be good if we would give thanks to God each day for loving us so much that he sent Jesus. Give thanks to Jesus for doing the will of the Father and going to the cross. Thank God for sending the Holy Spirit to dwell in us.

Prayer: Thank you, Father, Son and Holy Spirit, for all you have done for us. Amen

Esther Chapter 9

"Doing what Mordecai had written to them" (Esther 9:23 NIV).

"Do whatever he tells you" (John 2:5 NIV).

Are we doing what Jesus has told us to do?

Jesus and his disciples were at a wedding. Jesus' mother Mary was there also. It was the third day of the wedding celebration. Mary told Jesus that they had run out of wine. He tried to put her off. Mary wasn't offended; she told the servers to do whatever Jesus told them. She was confident he would meet the need. Jesus told the servers to fill the water jars with water. The servers filled the jars to the very top. Then he told them to take some to the host of the banquet, and the water was wine when the host drank it. (See John 2:1-10.)

The servers did what Jesus commanded them to do and there was a miracle. The servers didn't work the miracle; Jesus did. But he used the servers; they did their part.

Prayer: Lord, may we do our part and obey you, so you can do a miracle. Amen

Day 345

"Because *Haman* the son of Hammedatha, the Agagite, *the enemy* of all the Jews, *had devised against the Jews to destroy them,* and had cast Pur, that is, the lot, to consume them, and to destroy them" (Esther 9:24 KJV).

"Forgive ... in order that Satan might not outwit us. For we are not unaware of his schemes" (2 Corinthians 2:10-11 NIV).

Our enemy Satan plots against the church to destroy it. One way it can be threatened is from within. In Proverbs 6:16-19, there is a short list of things the Lord hates. One that made the short list is: the Lord hates those who cause division and conflict among people. We need to keep our eyes on Jesus, forgive the failings of others (not broadcast them), and carry on, doing what we sense the Lord is telling us to do.

In John 17:20-23, Jesus prayed for unity in his church, that the church would operate as one just as God and Jesus function as one. God entrusted the incredible message of salvation to be delivered by the church—imperfect believers.

When you get angry, be careful not to sin. Forgive a person quickly so that the devil won't have an opening and take advantage of you by causing division and discord in the church. (See Ephesians 4:26-27.)

Prayer: Lord, may we work together to shine your light brightly in the world. Amen

Day 346

"But when the plot came to the king's attention, he issued written orders that *the evil scheme Haman had devised* against the Jews *should come back onto his own head,* and that he and his sons should be impaled on poles" (Esther 9:25 NIV).

If a man maliciously digs a pit, he will fall in himself; if he in spite rolls a stone, it will come back on him. (See Proverbs 26:27.)

Haman was going to impale innocent Mordecai on a pole, and now Haman and his sons would be impaled on poles.

Isaac's son Jacob deceived his blind father by pretending to be his older brother Esau in order that he might receive the blessing of the elder son. Jacob had already tricked Esau out of his elder son birthright. Later Jacob married Rachel but was deceived by Rachel's father. On the wedding night, Rachel's father slipped older sister Leah into the tent instead of Rachel. Now Jacob had Leah as a wife. A week later he was given Rachel. (See Genesis 27-29.) Jacob the deceiver was deceived. You get what you give. (See Galatians 6:7.)

Jesus said it this way: Show mercy and you will receive mercy in return. Forgive and you also will be forgiven. Don't judge others and you won't be judged. Treat others the way you want to be treated. (See Matthew 5:7, 6:14, 7:1, 12.)

Prayer: Lord, help us to see that treating others right helps us as much as it does them. Amen

Day 347

"(Therefore these days were called Purim, from the word *pur.*) Because of everything written in this letter and because of *what they had seen and what had happened to them*" (Esther 9:26 NIV).

"For we cannot [help] but speak [about] the things which we have seen and heard" (Acts 4:20 KJV).

The disciples had witnessed many miracles Jesus had performed while here on earth. Later, when Peter and John encountered a lame man, they healed him in Jesus's name. When a crowd gathered, they began preaching about Jesus and his death and resurrection.

May we speak more and more about the things we have seen and heard the Lord do. What an encouragement and a faith builder it is to hear (or read) testimonies of the way God has worked in a person's life. One story may tell about a healing or a miraculous deliverance from trouble. Another might be the account of a person's life transformed by the power of God. Even daily small acts of God in our lives are worth sharing with others—for his glory.

Prayer: Lord, help us to tell others about the good things you do. Amen

Esther Chapter 9

Day 348

"The Jews took it on themselves to establish the custom that they and their descendants and all who join them should without fail observe these two days every year, in the way prescribed and at the time appointed" (Esther 9:27 NIV).

"Jesus died and rose again" (1 Thessalonians 4:14 KJV).

Yearly and without fail Christians observe these two events—the death and resurrection of our Lord and Savior, Jesus Christ. Part of that observance involves Holy Communion, where we identify with Christ and his sacrifice for us on the cross.

"The cup of blessing which we bless, is it not the communion of the blood of Christ? The bread which we brake, is it not the communion of the body of Christ?" (1 Corinthians 10:16 KJV).

The scripture says before you take the bread and cup you should examine yourself first. Make sure things are right between you and God or else you will be disciplined by the Lord. (See 1 Corinthians 11:23-32.)

When we have communion, and anytime we remember it—let's thank the Lord for his body broken for us and his blood shed for us.

Prayer: Lord, may we receive the elements of the bread and cup after we have made all things right with you. Amen

Day 349

"These days should be remembered and observed in every generation by every family, and in every province and in every city. And these days of Purim should never fail to be celebrated by the Jews—nor should the memory of these days die out among their descendants" (Esther 9:28 NIV).

"For whenever you eat this bread and drink this cup, you proclaim the Lord's death until he comes" (I Corinthians 11:26 NIV).

In every generation, the church is to remember Christ's death and celebrate his resurrection until he comes again.

In Noah's day, people went about their normal routine: eating, drinking and getting married. Then Noah and his family went into the ark and the flood came. Everyone else got washed away. (See Genesis 7:23.)

Also, in Lot's day everyone was going about their usual business; but once Lot got out of Sodom, the Lord sent down fire and destroyed all of them. (See Genesis 19:23-24.)

It will be like that when the Lord returns. People will be living their normal lives when one will be taken and the other left standing. Be ready, because we don't know when the Lord will come. (See Luke 17:26-35; Matthew 24:37-44.)

Jesus said, "Surely I come quickly. Amen" (Revelation 22:20 KJV).

Prayer: Lord, when you return, may you find us ready. Amen

Esther Chapter 9

"Then Esther the queen, the daughter of Abihail, *and Mordecai the Jew,* wrote *with all authority,* to confirm this second letter of Purim" (Esther 9:29 KJV).

"All authority in heaven and on earth has been given to me" (Matthew 28:18 NIV).

"Then [Jesus] called his twelve disciples together, and gave them power and authority" (Luke 9:1 KJV). Jesus had the authority to cast out devils and heal diseases; he gave the same authority to the disciples. He also sent them to the different towns to preach about the kingdom of God.

Has God's agenda changed for his disciples of today? There are still people who need to be delivered, people who need healing and people who need to hear about the kingdom of God.

Prayer: Lord, raise up disciples that will go in the power and authority of your name. Amen

Day 351

"*And Mordecai sent letters to all* the Jews in the 127 provinces of Xerxes' kingdom– *words of goodwill and assurance*" (Esther 9:30 NIV).

Jesus said, "I am with you [always], even unto the end of the world" (Matthew 28:20 KJV).

Jesus also spoke these words of assurance:

"Peace I leave with you, my peace I give unto you: not as the world [gives], give I unto you, Let not your heart be troubled, neither let it be afraid" (John 14:27 KJV).

"In the world [you] shall have tribulation: but be of good cheer; I have overcome the world" (John 16:33 KJV).

"With God all things are possible" (Mark 10:27 KJV).

"If the Son therefore shall make you free, [you] shall be free indeed" (John 8:36 KJV).

"I am the resurrection, and the life: he that [believes] in me, though he were dead, yet shall he live" (John 11:25 KJV).

"I go to prepare a place for you. ... I will come again, and receive you unto myself; that where I am, there [you] may be also" (John 14:2-3 KJV).

Prayer: Lord, thank you for your peace and for the assurance that you are always with us. Amen

Esther Chapter 9

Day 352

"To establish these days of Purim at their designated times, as Mordecai the Jew and Queen Esther had decreed for them, and as *they had established for themselves and their descendants* in regard to their times of fasting and lamentation" (Esther 9:31 NIV).

The Jews and their descendants were also to observe the Passover: the time the Lord "passed over the houses of the children of Israel in Egypt" (Exodus 12:27 KJV).

At the first Passover, the Israelites slaughtered lambs and used the blood to put on the doorframes of their homes. This was so the death angel would "pass over" and spare them. (In the Egyptians' houses, without the blood on the doorpost, the firstborn perished.)

Christ was crucified during the Passover celebration. He was the Passover lamb; his blood was shed to be applied to our hearts, so that the death angel will pass over us and we will be spared—for eternity.

John the Baptist proclaimed that Jesus was the Lamb of God who came to take the world's sin away. (See John 1:29.)

In heaven, thousands of angels were "saying with a loud voice, Worthy is the Lamb that was slain to receive power, and riches, and wisdom, and strength, and [honor] and glory, and blessing" (Revelation 5:12 KJV).

Prayer: Lamb of God, you are worthy of all glory and honor and power. Amen

Day 353

"And the decree of Esther confirmed these matters of Purim; and it was written in the book" (Esther 9:32 KJV).

"Now I say that Jesus Christ was a minister ... for the truth of God, to confirm the promises made unto the fathers [of the faith]: And that the Gentiles might glorify God for his mercy. ... There shall be a root of Jesse [referring to Christ], and he ... shall rise to reign over the Gentiles; in him shall the Gentiles trust" (Romans 15:8-9, 12 KJV).

Christ himself has confirmed the promises of old, so that we may believe and have God's mercy. In his mercy he has also included those who are not Jews—the Gentiles!

The Jews are God's chosen people. They are the ones to whom God sent the prophets so that they might know him. Through the Jews—and one Gentile, Luke—we have the written word of God. But God in his mercy has given salvation to all; Jews and non-Jews alike, if they believe on his Son.

Prayer: Lord, thank you that all the people of the world may know you as their Savior and Lord. Amen

Chapter 9 Review

Day 308: We have a powerful force to use against those determined to destroy us: prayer!

Day 319: May we give the Lord control of our lives, and let God be "God" in other people's lives, not us.

Day 320: Lord, help us let go of stuff we don't need.

Day 324: Let's be patient and wait on his timing.

Day 332: Storing up treasure on earth is about getting; storing up treasure in heaven is about giving.

Day 333: We need to get away somewhere quiet and alone with Jesus to get rest for our bodies and souls.

Day 340: We have been set free from sin, not to look better in the eyes of others, or to feel better about ourselves, but to live holy lives before God and do his will.

Prayer: God, may we surrender everything to you. Amen

Day 355

Chapter 9 Challenge

Fill in the blank.

1. The _____ were able to overcome their enemies. (9:1)

2. _____ became more and more famous in the kingdom. (9:4)

3. The Jews struck down their enemies with the _____. (9:5)

4. The Jews in other areas of the kingdom _____ to protect themselves. (9:16)

5. After their victory they had a celebration with _____ and _____. (9:17-19)

6. When they observed these days, they were to give _____ and _____ to the poor. (9:22)

7. They called these days of celebration _____. (9:28)

Prayer: Lord, may we celebrate you daily. Amen

"King Xerxes imposed tribute throughout the empire, to its distant shores" (Esther 10:1 NIV).

"Bring... all the tithes into the storehouse" (Malachi 3:10 KJV).

The tribute represents the tithe. Tithing is giving the Lord ten percent of what he has given to us. God said the Israelites were robbing him by not giving him their tithes and offerings. He promised them he would bless them greatly if they would give him what he required. (See Malachi 3:7-12.)

Jesus mentioned tithing when he was rebuking the scribes and Pharisees. He said they paid tithes even down to the smallest amounts of herbs, but they failed to do the most important things in the law, like justice, mercy and faith; they should have done both. (See Matthew 23:23.)

Paul doesn't use the word tithe, but he mentions that others were getting financial support for preaching the gospel and he asked different churches to take up weekly collections to help the saints. (See 1 Corinthians 16:1-2.)

Prayer: Lord, help us to be willing to give to you and trust you to provide for us. Amen

Day 357

"And all his acts of power and might" (Esther 10:2 NIV).

"Power and might are in your hand, and no one can withstand you" (2 Chronicles 20:6, NIV).

Here is one example of God's power and might:

Jehoshaphat, king of Judah, was told that a huge enemy army was coming after his people. He called for a fast and the people came together to seek the Lord and ask for his help. The Spirit of God came upon one man and he spoke a word from the Lord. He said,

"Be not afraid nor dismayed by reason of this great multitude; for the battle is not yours, but God's" (2 Chronicles 20:15 KJV).

The next morning the king sent out a choir ahead of the army to praise the Lord. When they started to sing songs of praise to the Lord, God had the enemy army fight among themselves and all the enemy soldiers were killed. The other countries feared God when they heard how the Lord had destroyed the enemies of Israel. (See 2 Chronicles 20.)

Prayer: Lord, may we praise you ahead of time for the victory you will perform in our midst. Amen

"Together with a full account of the greatness of Mordecai" (Esther 10:2 NIV).

"Since I myself have carefully investigated everything from the beginning, I too decided to write an orderly account for you" (Luke 1:3 NIV)

When Jesus was about thirty years old, he was baptized by John and led into the desert by the Holy Spirit to be tempted by the devil. He resisted the devil's enticements. He lived his whole life without sinning; he always did what was right. (See Hebrews 4:15; 1 Peter 2:22.)

Jesus began his earthly ministry by teaching in the Jewish synagogues and working miracles. Luke recorded that: "The blind see, the lame walk, the lepers are cleansed, the deaf hear, the dead are raised, [and] to the poor the gospel is preached" (Luke 7:22 KJV). He called twelve men to follow him; he taught them and trained them to assist him in his ministry.

After about three years, he was betrayed by one of his disciples, arrested and crucified. He died for the sins of all humanity. After three days he rose from the dead and appeared to his disciples on many occasions. Jesus imparted a blessing to his disciples and was then taken up into heaven.

This is not a full account, but just a few of the great things Jesus did on the earth.

Prayer: Thank you, Jesus, for coming to live among us and doing great things for us. Amen

Day 359

"Whom the king had promoted" (Esther 10:2 NIV).
"God ... [has] highly exalted him" (Philippians 2:9 KJV).

Mordecai was promoted by the king. Jesus was promoted by the Father.

"God ... [has] highly exalted him, and given him a name which is above every name: That at the name of Jesus every knee should bow, of things in heaven, and things in earth, and things under the earth; And that every tongue should confess that Jesus Christ is Lord, to the glory of God the Father" (Philippians 2:9-11 KJV).

This same highly exalted Jesus loves us, forgives us, hears our prayers and answers them. He comforts us in our sorrows and is our friend. He came and rescued us from sin so that we could spend eternity with him. We can count on him to keep his promises because he is the same now and forever. (See Hebrews 13:8.) He is worthy of our praise, adoration and dedication.

Prayer: Jesus, you are above all things and we worship you. Amen

"Are they *not written in the book* of the annals of the kings of Media and Persia?" (Esther 10:2 NIV).

"And there are also many other things which Jesus did ... which, if they should be written every one, I suppose that even the world itself could not contain the books that should be written. Amen" (John 21:25 KJV).

Here are a few things that Jesus did while on the earth as recorded in the Book of Matthew:

Jesus began preaching and called people to repent and turn from their sins. (4:17)

He taught people about the kingdom of God. (Chapter 5-)

A man with leprosy came to Jesus and he healed him. (8:2-3)

Jesus and his disciples were on a lake when a terrible storm came up. He spoke to the storm and it became calm. (8:23-27)

He healed a paralyzed man; raised a girl from the dead; healed two blind men and one who was mute. (Chapter 9)

Jesus fed over five thousand people (14:15-21) and later fed over four thousand (15:32-38) with only a few fish and a few loaves of bread.

He died for the sins of all people, and those who believe in him will live with God forever. (Chapter 27)

Prayer: Lord, you are able to do anything; nothing is too hard for you. Amen

Day 361

"Mordecai the Jew was second in rank to King Xerxes" (Esther 10:3 NIV).

"And the head of Christ is God" (1 Corinthians 11:3 KJV).

Jesus submitted to God's authority and came to the earth.

From the Book of John:

Jesus said he came to do the will of the Father. The Father sent him and he was to complete the work the Father had for him to do. (4:34)

He came down from heaven to do God's will and not his own. God's will was that Jesus not lose those the Father had given him but on the last day raise them up. (6:38-39)

Jesus didn't come by his own authority—God sent him. And he knows the Father because he had come from being with him in heaven. (7:28-29)

Jesus said God loved him because he was going to lay down his life for the sheep. God had commanded him to lay down his life and had given him authority to raise it up. (10:17-18)

He brought glory to the Father by doing what he was sent to do. (17:4)

Prayer: Thank you Lord, for doing the will of the Father. Amen

"Preeminent among the Jews" (Esther 10:3 NIV).

"And he is the head of the body, the church ... that in all things he might have the preeminence" (Colossians 1:18 KJV).

Jesus was remarkable, the highest quality of a man and he far surpassed anyone who had ever lived. He was kind and compassionate to the hurting but strongly opposed those who used their "religious" position as a means of power and prestige. As head of the church, he is the example that we should follow. All the qualities of God himself resided in Christ, and he lived his life showing the world what the Father was like.

As our head directs our thoughts, words and deeds, so should Christ as the head of the "body of Christ," direct the church. All church leaders and members answer to him—he is above all authorities and powers in the church and outside it.

Prayer: Jesus, may the Church be under your leadership and authority. Amen

Day 363

"And held in high esteem by his many fellow Jews" (Esther 10:3 NIV).

"And daily in the temple, and in every house, they ceased not to teach and preach Jesus Christ" (Acts 5:42 KJV).

When Peter preached about the death and resurrection of Christ to the crowd, on the day of Pentecost, the Holy Spirit convicted their hearts. Peter told them to turn from their sins and receive forgiveness from God. That day three thousand people were saved. Later, thousands more were added to the church. The message of Jesus continued to spread and many priests came to believe in Christ. (See Acts 2, 4:4, 6:7.)

Today people meet in churches, homes, fields, wherever they can, so they can hear about Jesus because they hold him in high esteem. He has changed their lives, forgiven their sins and given them hope.

Prayer: Lord, you are worthy of all praise. Amen

Day 364

"Because [Mordecai] worked for the good of his people and spoke up for the welfare of all the Jews" (Esther 10:3 NIV).

"And we know that all things work together for good to them that love God, to them who are the called according to his purpose" (Romans 8:28 KJV).

Jesus is working for the good of his people—to make them good, holy and righteous. Christ has "saved us, and called us with [a] holy calling, not according to our works, but according to his own purpose" (2 Timothy 1:9 KJV).

Our holy calling is to be like Jesus. Our purpose in life is to do his will. Christ wants us to give ourselves to him so he can make us holy. We are not to conform to the standards of this world. He wants to transform us on the inside so that we can be a bride worthy of him.

Prayer: Lord, make us holy and pleasing to you so that we can be your Bride. Amen and Amen

To the reader:

"The Spirit and the bride say, 'Come!' And let the one who hears say, 'Come!' Let the one who is thirsty come; and let the one who wishes take the free gift of the water of life" (Revelation 22:17 NIV).

Day 365

Chapter 10 Review

Day 357: Lord, may we praise you ahead of time for the victory.

Day 359: This same highly exalted Jesus loves us, forgives us, hears our prayers and answers them.

Day 360: Lord, you are able to do anything; nothing is too hard for you.

Day 364: Our holy calling is to be like Jesus.

Chapter 10 Challenge

Fill in the blank.

1. The king _____ all the land. (10:1)

2. _____ was second in rank to the king. (10:3)

3. He was held in high esteem because he worked for the good of the _____. (10:3)

Prayer: Thank you, Lord; you are working for our good. Amen